UNPLUG

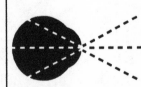 This Large Print Book carries the
Seal of Approval of N.A.V.H.

Unplug

A SIMPLE GUIDE TO MEDITATION FOR BUSY SKEPTICS AND MODERN SOUL SEEKERS

Suze Yalof Schwartz
with Debra Goldstein

THORNDIKE PRESS

A part of Gale, Cengage Learning

GALE
CENGAGE Learning·

Farmington Hills, Mich • San Francisco • New York • Waterville, Maine
Meriden, Conn • Mason, Ohio • Chicago

Copyright © 2017 by Suzanne Yalof Schwartz.
Thorndike Press, a part of Gale, Cengage Learning.

LIBRARY OF CONGRESS CIP DATA ON FILE.
CATALOGING-IN-PUBLICATION FOR THIS BOOK
IS AVAILABLE FROM THE LIBRARY OF CONGRESS.

ISBN: 978-1-4328-4049-5 (hardcover)
ISBN: 1-4328-4049-5 (hardcover)

Published in 2017 by arrangement with Harmony Books, an imprint of
Crown Publishing Group, a division of Penguin Random House, LLC

Printed in Mexico
1 2 3 4 5 6 7 21 20 19 18 17

To my husband, Marc, my true love and the expediter of all of my dreams. Thank you for granting me full access to your brilliant mind, for your constant support, and for your love and kindness always.

To my boys:
You keep life light, fun, and challenging and remind me to breathe!

CONTENTS

READY, SET, UNPLUG

Almost everything will work again if you unplug it for a few minutes, including you.

— ANNE LAMOTT

The minute I learned to unplug, my whole life changed. Little did I know that nearly five years later I would be on a mission to convince you to join me. But when you discover a life hack this good, you want to share it with as many people as you can! By learning to unplug, I stepped off the crazy roller coaster of stress and into a life in which I'm calm and in control (well, most of the time). I'm getting more done and doing it so much better because I'm focused and clear, and enjoying it a million times more because I'm present. I wrote this book to teach you how to unplug and meditate so you, too, can experience and enjoy your life as it's actually happening instead of missing out on the good stuff because of worry,

9

anxiety, and busyness. There's no reason to walk around with stress when getting rid of it is so simple.

Every day, I have people asking me to help them learn how to meditate. There are so many confusing resources out there, so I created the highly curated, give-it-to-me-straight, definitive guide I wish I'd had when I first started out. Having taken hundreds of hours of classes, tried every form of meditation, and launched the first drop-in meditation studio, I can say I totally get the art of meditation. The good news for you is that there isn't much to get — it's not complicated! I wrote this for all of you who want to learn to meditate but think it's too complicated, too weird, that you don't have the time, or that you couldn't possibly sit still for even a few minutes a day. Believe me, I get it — I was the least likely person to become a meditator! But as one of my high school classmates said at our thirty-year reunion, "If Yalof can meditate, anyone can." So even if you think it will be impossible for me to get you to do it, I'm ready to take the challenge and make it *un*challenging for you.

Before I started my journey, I would have laughed if you'd told me that the key to being effective, productive, happier, and more successful isn't to go faster, do more, try harder, but to slow down and get present. I was a classic type A personality and over-achiever: insanely busy, impatient, and racing through my life at two hundred miles an hour. I thrived on the fast pace and demands of my busy life, and I attacked every opportunity that came my way with enthusiasm. Pausing to breathe and ask myself whether I should or shouldn't do so wasn't even on my radar, and *no* wasn't in my vocabulary. If something wasn't going right, I would still find a way to *make* it work. Or, more accurately, I would make my assistants find a way to make it work, which would stress them out and sometimes make them cry. It's no surprise that when the *New York Times* published an article about my meditation studio, Unplug, I saw a comment on my former assistant's Facebook feed that said, "I wish she was meditating when we worked for her" (Sorry, Lexa!).

The thought of sitting still seemed not only impossible and like torture, but a total waste of time. How could I possibly think about unplugging for even a few minutes a day when there was so much to do and so much I needed to accomplish?

But now I know I could have gotten to the top much quicker and loved the whole process a lot more if I'd learned how to slow down and unplug. Ironic, right? Do less, accomplish more. Get calm to get ahead. All we have to do is sit still for a few minutes a day to find the holy grail of peace, happiness, and high-level life success we're chasing.

That's not just my opinion — there's serious science to back me up here. Studies have proven that meditation is the secret sauce to being healthier, happier, and way more effective. It physically rewires your brain to make you smarter and more focused, productive, and positive. It reduces anxiety, stress, panic attacks, anger, depression, overeating, and pain. It improves your memory, helps you make better and faster decisions, increases compassion, and gives you a serious edge on handling the challenges life throws your way. It helps clear away the clutter and chaos in your brain that lead to the clutter and chaos in your life, so everything just flows better.

I know this sounds like a lot of big promises, but I have seen it work on thousands of people — many of them skeptics at first. There's a reason why thirty million Americans are meditating daily! Make that number thirty million and one if you start right now. It is the one practice that actually works for *anyone* willing to commit to it. After five years of doing it almost daily I still can't believe that stopping to do nothing is so huge.

That's why I want you to discover this life-changing secret. It changes your whole existence for the better. Not only does it make you calmer, healthier, and more productive, it also helps you answer the bigger, deeper questions like *What makes me happy?* and *What do I want?* And sometimes, as it did for me, unplugging and getting present leads you to the life you were meant to be living.

I spent two decades racing to the top of the ladder in the world of fashion. I worked at *Vogue, Elle, Marie Claire,* and, eventually, at *Glamour* magazine, where I styled photo shoots, covered the famous "Do's and Don'ts" section and became known (according to the *New York Times,* at least) as "The Fairy Godmother of Makeovers." I traveled the country doing makeovers for *The Oprah Winfrey Show,* the *Today* show, *Good Morning America,* and many others. I also covered the red carpet during awards shows and the fashion shows in New York, Paris, Milan, and London, both front and backstage. It was hectic and I loved it!

There were some pretty crazy moments,

but I never thought about "stress management," because, honestly, I was too excited by what I was doing to think about whether I was stressed. I loved my life, pressure and all. So what if decompressing meant circling the office schmoozing as a cover to casually reach into people's candy jars?

I tore through my daily to-do lists, scattered and crazed. Even though I always prided myself on being a positive and happy person, I still had the tendency to rush everyone around me, lose focus easily, obsess over silly things, blow up at my kids and husband from time to time, and get über-stressed on deadlines. Not attractive! I compensated by moving faster and faster and sheepishly apologizing later.

I had a glamorous job, a terrific husband, and three great kids. But what I didn't have was the ability to appreciate the present moment. In my hurry to get to the next thing, I sped through each one, hardly ever landing in the one I was in. I was having all these major moments between my job and my family life, but missing out on most of them because I was on to the next one immediately upon arrival. I zipped through my life in such high gear that I didn't get how much was passing me by, all the richness I was missing out on. You don't realize you're just skating on the surface when your life is just a series of checklists.

Fast forward to the summer of 2010, when the LA-based job opportunity of a lifetime landed in the lap of my husband, Marc, and so my family and I moved to California to pursue our next adventure.

I don't think I really anticipated the culture shock I'd feel moving from Manhattan, which felt like the middle of everything, to California, which has a much different vibe and daily pace of life. But the bigger shock was going from having what I thought was an exciting job to wondering what I was doing with my life, in this new place, with new everything. I had always worked and I honestly did not know what to do with myself without a job. My kids were in school all day and I found myself filling the time with window shopping, bracelet beading classes, grocery store visits, and lunches and breakfasts. I was not only bored and restless — I was getting fat! I kept getting offers to go back into fashion, but nothing felt quite right until Lord & Taylor called to hire me to film Taxi TV commercials. It was a great gig with plenty of round-trip tickets to NYC, so I said yes. I was thrilled to be back in action. Yet something felt different this time.

Between navigating a bicoastal commute, setting up a new life in a new town, juggling the lives of three fun and highly energetic little boys while on the road, and spending time with my husband, I experienced a moment in which I felt an overwhelming sense of stress. For the first time I could remember, I realized that I actually *couldn't* do it all. I wasn't in crisis, exactly — this was just normal life stress that got amped up, the way it does for so many of us. But that everyday stress, as you know, is enough to overwhelm you and send you over the edge.

Fortunately, I voiced this to the right person at just the right time. My mother-in-law, who is a psychotherapist, said, "Let me show you a little trick." She told me to close my eyes and taught me how to calm myself down instantly using my breath and visualization. In just three minutes, I went from feeling completely stressed to feeling totally calm. It was amazing!

As soon as I opened my eyes, three things went through my head:

1. I can't believe how easy and simple that was.
2. Why had I not known about this secret before?
3. I want more! Who can teach me? How? Where?!?

My mother-in-law suggested I learn to meditate, so I went on a search to find the best place. I started by googling "places to meditate in Los Angeles" and found out there was nowhere I could go to just pop in, learn, and leave. There was a fourteen-hundred-dollar Transcendental Meditation course; a four-day training intensive in a Vedic instructor's apartment; a six-week program at the UCLA Mindful Awareness Research Center. I was surprised that there wasn't a quicker or easier way to learn it.

The "aha moment" came when I thought, *Why can't there be a Drybar for meditation?* When you get your hair done at one of these salons that does exclusively blowouts, you go in feeling icky and come out feeling fabulous in thirty minutes or less. Check in, get it done, check out (I know, I'm still such a New Yorker). Why wasn't there a similar way for busy people to fit meditation into their lives? Why no popular method and no place where someone like me could learn without making a long-term commitment or spending a small fortune? I took to Google yet again to see if any such place existed. It didn't. Not in Los Angeles, and not in the entire United States. Not even in Europe or Asia. Then it hit me: Meditation needed a makeover, and I was just the one to do it.

Marc, ever the wise one, told me I should probably learn to meditate first. Right . . . there was that. So I committed 400 percent to cracking the code on this new discovery of mine and jumped in with both feet. I signed up for the program given by the distractingly hot Australian instructor (I swear, there's no such thing as an unattractive Vedic instructor) and went through the entire six-week program at UCLA. I took classes everywhere I could find them, from yoga studios to Buddhist temples to a meet-up group on the beach in Santa Monica. I did all of Deepak Chopra's 21-Day Meditations; downloaded the Headspace app; watched every podcast from Sharon Salzberg and Pema Chödrön to Tara Brach; and read everything I could get my hands on by Thich Nhat Hanh, Robert Thurman, Dan Siegel, Jon Kabat-Zinn, Joseph Goldstein, Eckhart Tolle, the Maharishi Mahesh Yogi, Davidji, Steve Ross, and Olivia Rosewood. While I was learning how to unplug from the chaos of my daily life for a little while, I became an accidental meditation connoisseur.

I fell in love with so many different styles and techniques and so many teachers during that time. But, at the same time, my makeover brain kept wanting to edit the teachers' content, the ultraslow pace, the wardrobes, the spaces, the instructors' "meditation-y" voices, the heavy sage burning and chanting, the long stories meant to illustrate a point, the Q&A afterward that kept you trapped for an additional forty-five minutes and felt more like a group therapy session . . . the whole experience. Meditation is so simple, and I couldn't figure out why so much of it was being presented as so heady and complex — or worse, boring and unnecessarily drawn out. I remember one teacher taking a five-second pause between (pause) every (pause) word (pause) in his opening talk. I found it so frustrating!

I wanted an experience that someone like me could actually sit through — to cut through all the excess and curate the best of meditation teachings, kind of like a brilliantly produced morning television segment. Every television segment takes roughly five minutes to inspire, explain the why, how to, and give solid tips so that by the end of the piece, you get it and can go do it. That's how I felt learning to meditate should be.

Hello, Unplug!

I started Unplug, the world's first secular drop-in meditation studio, to share meditation in its simplest, cleanest form. I wanted to take the practice from esoteric to accessible and create a place that would apply to busy, modern people so they could unplug from life for even just a few minutes a day, recharge, and experience the undeniable effects of meditation.

Meditation has changed me and my life in so many ways. I am much more able to see when I'm stressed and deal with it in that exact moment, rather than being consumed or overwhelmed by it. I was always a happy person, but now I'm happy and grateful because I stop to appreciate everything around me. I am so much more effective and productive. I used to do a lot; the difference is that now I do it in a more focused way, so I get more done in less time. I'm doing ten times more but I do it consciously, so everything is better. I used to avoid things that made me feel uncomfortable, but now I can handle any discomfort. Even when things aren't going right, I'm able to go with the flow rather than feel frustrated. In almost every situation, I can step back from my knee-jerk reactions and respond mindfully, which makes me a better mom, wife, and boss.

But most of all, I don't miss out on moments anymore. That's the big payoff. Whatever I'm doing or whoever I'm with, I am actually present — not off in my head thinking about what happened yesterday or what I need to do later. When I take a brain hike, I notice it quicker and bring myself back. I look people in the eye and really hear and see them. Food tastes better, colors look brighter. The best way I can describe it is that I feel like I'm experiencing my life in high def.

But enough about me. This book is about you, and how you can improve your life by unplugging via meditation in just minutes a day. I'm guessing you picked up this book because you've heard all about the power of meditation and want to learn how to do it — just without the mysticism and woo-woo stuff that usually comes along with it. And that's exactly what I'm going to give to you. You are going to learn to meditate in under five minutes, and you'll feel the results immediately.

I'm on a mission to prove that everyone — including you — can meditate. Even if — no, *especially* if — you believe you think too much, have no time, can't sit still, or that it's just not you. I've seen with my own eyes the high-powered trader whose daily panic attacks stopped after he started meditating, and the big, burly tattooed personal trainer whose serious traffic-induced anger issues vanished. I've met a woman who went through three unsuccessful rounds of in vitro fertilization, finally getting pregnant on the fourth round after she began a regular meditation practice. I've talked to former insomniacs who are now sleeping peacefully through the night and countless chronic pain patients sent to us from UCLA who swear meditating is better than Percocet. I've seen some of the most stressed people go from anxious to serene, from pinched and drawn to smiling and radiant. These are the stories that I hear every day — usually accompanied by big tears of relief and huge hugs.

You'll start out in "Take a Seat," where I'll give you a quick tutorial on what's in it for you if you learn to unplug. I'll explain what meditation is and what it isn't, and I'll debunk a lot of the misperceptions floating around out there — starting with the notion that you need to turn off your brain or sit perfectly still for long periods of time for it to work. Completely untrue. I'll also let you in on all the incredible benefits you'll experience, along with all the proof and science to back up exactly how and why meditation works.

Then, in "Unplug and Recharge," I'll give you Unplug's signature Simple Formula for

Straight-Up Meditation, along with other tools and techniques so you can easily incorporate this practice into your daily life. Throughout, you'll find lots of tips from wise, insightful, funny, and inspiring meditation teachers as well as folks I've met throughout my journey. I'll also give you the how-to on other meditation methods to try, along with some quick-hit meditations you can use whenever you need them throughout your day. These will be like your secret stash of instant serenity and bliss! There's the Espresso Meditation, for when you find yourself in a pressure cooker situation and need to get calm and unplug . . . fast! There's the Starbucks Meditation, which is a super-simple way to start your day off in a present, mindful way. Then, of course, there's one of my favorites: the Feel the Love Meditation, for when someone really drives you crazy and you need to cool down.

In "Keep It Going," I'll tell you about a few other meditation-related practices you might want to explore, like sound baths (the coolest experience *ever*), crystal healing (way more grounded than you think), and meditation for kids (changed my life as a parent). And — of course — it'll all be concise and completely accessible.

A few months ago, I was being interviewed by a reporter for a television segment. We were talking about our method of condensing and simplifying mindfulness meditation practice, and she asked me with a note of disdain in her voice, "Okay, but isn't this turning the practice of meditation into Mc-Mindfulness?"

My answer? "I hope so, because I want everyone to be able to take a bite!"

Bon appétit, friends. Let's go get you unplugged.

■ ■ ■ ■

TAKE A SEAT

■ ■ ■ ■

Come on in. Pull up a cushion. This is my streamlined introduction to unplugging. I'll tell you exactly what meditation is and what it isn't, how it works, what you can expect to happen, and exactly how and why it will dramatically change your life.

No fuss, no fluff. Easy and simple — just like meditation.

YOU, UNPLUGGED

It was a typical day for me in my life as an editor at *Glamour*. I'd flown in from New York early that morning to do a fashion makeover on female NASCAR fans right there in the pit. With only a few hours to get this right, we were on a tight schedule, plus *Good Morning America* was filming the makeovers for a segment. But I wasn't worried — the tighter the schedule and the higher the stakes, the faster I moved.

I was zipping through the preparations until I pulled out the bag of clothing my assistant had packed up to bring with us. The instant I saw what was in the bag, I knew we were in trouble. She had packed the wrong stuff. Not just a few pieces — the entire collection was the reject rack that my boss had said, very clearly and emphatically, "DO NOT TAKE." Not good. This shoot was costing the magazine at least $50,000 between the flights, hotels, location vans, and more, plus we were slotted to be on live television; needless to say, it would be very bad and would all come down on me if this didn't happen.

Okay, I thought, trying to stay calm. *We'll get some replacement clothes from a nearby store and save this.* I was still in high-gear fix-it mode right up until the moment I found out the closest store that sold clothing was a Sears twenty miles away. That's when the panic kicked in. I felt the blood rushing to my face, and my heart started hammering wildly. And then I just lost it.

First I started yelling. I'm not proud to admit this, but mostly at my assistant. Then I went into the bathroom and cried. I know we're talking about a fashion shoot, so to most this all might seem a little frivolous, but I felt like my entire career was on the line. I felt sick.

Finally, after thirty minutes of sky-high stress, panic, and mayhem, I got my head back on straight and quickly turned it into a beauty shoot in which we'd only feature the participants from the neck up. The shoot was saved, but I couldn't take back the emotional collateral damage I'd caused for myself and for my assistant. I packed up the shoot that day feeling drained, remorseful, and downright embarrassed.

Fast forward to last month, a typical gorgeous, sunny Thursday afternoon in Los Angeles. I'd just finished leading a private meditation group and was in a great mood. Another teacher was about to begin the midday class, so I went into my office in the back of the studio to do some paperwork. A few minutes into the class, I heard very loud noises coming from the street. The studio is right on Wilshire Boulevard, a busy main street, so it wasn't unusual to hear sounds, but these were different from normal street noises. So my manager, Deborah, and I went outside to see what was going on.

Right outside our building, we saw two police officers crouched dramatically, the way you see on crime shows, pointing guns directly in our faces toward the bank next door. They yelled to us to go back inside immediately, lock the doors, and stay away from the windows. Instantaneously, I felt that same total and utter panic flood through me. I was totally freaked out. Judging from the look on Deborah's pale, shocked face, I could tell she felt the same way.

We ran back inside and quickly locked the door. It took roughly three seconds before my training kicked in and I said to Deborah, "We need to breathe." We took three long, slow breaths and immediately down-shifted from freaked-out to calm. I then walked back into the studio, where nineteen students were blissed out and totally un-aware of what was happening outside. I interrupted the class and explained what was going on, and brought everyone to the back room, where there were no windows. Yes, it was scary to think that bullets could come flying through the walls or windows, but I stayed completely calm and, as a result, kept everyone else calm.

That day — when I faced a genuine, potentially dangerous crisis — I didn't lose my cool. I didn't panic and, in turn, panic everyone around me. I didn't make a bad situation worse by ramping up the stress. Instead, I stayed focused and in control and walked away from that crisis feeling proud, productive, and peaceful.

After about an hour, the police came to the door and told us everything was now "Code 4," which meant that all was okay. Even though the robbers had escaped with the money from the bank, no one was hurt, and we could go back to business as usual.

I'm telling you this story because that's exactly what happens when you learn to unplug. It can turn your whole life into a Code 4, no matter what is going on. Work snafu or gun pointing in your direction, it doesn't matter: Your brain reacts the same way when it perceives a threat, and the biological fight-or-flight mechanism kicks in. The hammering heart, tense muscles, racing blood, narrowed focus, and all the rest are all your biochemistry's way of preparing you for a legitimate attack — it doesn't know if that attack is coming in the form of an angry boss or a flying bullet. Unplugging allows you to respond calmly and rationally and maintain your peace no matter which it is.

Think about how many minutes, hours, or days you've lost to a snag in your work or personal life. No matter how insignificant the event might seem to anyone else, to you it's *huge*. It rattles your emotions, steals your focus, triggers anything from headaches to acid stomach to worse, and often leaves you feeling guilty or embarrassed by how you reacted.

When you learn how to unplug, you take back control. You get to choose: thirty minutes of sky-high stress and — to borrow a phrase from the world-renowned meditation teacher Davidji — scorching the village around you to the ground (along with all the repercussions of that) or going from crazed to calm within three seconds and

31

saving yourself and the rest of the villagers. Having experienced both, I can promise you I'm never going back to the former.

Unplugging doesn't mean you shut down, run away, or check out. It isn't about "taking a breather" or zoning out. Going for a run, or reading a book, or getting a massage is relaxing, but that's not the kind of unplugging I'm talking about.

To unplug means to consciously unhook from whatever is amping you up (the perceived danger), reset, and restart from a neutral, empowered place. You consciously disconnect from the crazy current for a few minutes and recharge in a focused way to get where you want to go. It gives you the ability to consciously switch from panic to calm, anger to reason, sad to happy. Complicated problems will feel easier to solve. You'll be able to see clearly what you want, let go of obsessing and worrying, and quickly make decisions that are aligned with what truly matters to you. You'll have the power to resist pigging out and to keep your cool when your kid, or spouse, or boss, is driving you over the edge.

Can meditation really do all this? Yes. All you have to do is do it for a few minutes every day. It's just like going to the gym: If you keep doing it, you'll see the results. If you're skeptical, that's great — you *should* be asking what's in it for you! In the next few chapters, I'm going to tell you exactly what you can expect to happen and prove to you how much easier and nicer your life will be when you take control of your emotions, your reactions, and your mind.

What do you want to let go of? What do you want to gain? It'll all happen when you learn how to unplug and meditate.

WHAT IS MEDITATION?

Meditation is a practice that teaches you to unplug from distraction and experience the present moment.

Wait, that's it?

That's it. But hang on, because I'm going to tell you why that's such a big deal.

According to the National Science Foundation, the average person has approximately fifty thousand thoughts a day. The thoughts just keep coming, all day long, stealing our attention away from the present moment. The problem is, the present moment is kind of important, because it's where your life is actually happening. Not five minutes ago, not five minutes from now — right here, right now. That's all there is. We can ruminate on what happened yesterday or worry about what we need to do tomorrow . . . none of which is actually happening *in this moment*.

You know how those mini mental tornadoes go: *I have to pick up my dry cleaning . . . I wonder why they call it "dry cleaning" . . . I need to pick up dinner . . . What should I have for dinner . . . hmm, loved that Indian place I went to with Amy . . . I'd love to go to India one day . . . I wonder how Joe's trip was . . . I really need to call Joe . . .* Meditation experts call that jumping from thought to thought "monkey mind." I call it "Google Brain."

Other thoughts can trigger big, overwhelming feelings that really suck us in. This usually happens when we hit something unexpected. Something goes in a way other than we want, and we automatically go to our habituated (and usually not-so-calm) response. It goes something like this:

Your boss criticizes you: *What an idiot . . . I hate this job . . . my career sucks . . .*
You lose your wallet: *I'm an idiot . . . I never do anything right . . . I suck . . .*
You hit crazy traffic: *Everyone's an idiot . . . why do I live here . . . this city sucks . . .*

We're human; these automatic reactions are totally normal. The problem is that we're not only losing our cool — we're also losing our choice in the matter about how we respond. The thoughts and emotions take over and we feel powerless to stop them.

But I've got good news for you: Just because the crazy train pulls into the station doesn't necessarily mean you have to climb on board! There is a way to be in control of your reactions and emotions, rather than the other way around. True, we can't stop any of those fifty thousand thoughts from streaming in, habitual or otherwise. But through meditation, we train our brains to *let the ones that don't serve us pass right on by.* Meditation teaches you to consciously direct your attention where you want it to be, especially when you're off in distraction or reaction land. This is the act of unplugging. You do this while you're in your meditation so that it becomes an ingrained habit in your daily life. You cultivate your ability to direct your focus, and then *you* get to choose how you want to respond in every circumstance rather than feeling like a puppet at the mercy of your automatic wiring.

Meditation teacher Davidji has an analogy for this that I love. He compares our brains to cell phones with texts, e-mails, and other alerts streaming in all the time. When we train our brain through meditation, the thoughts still flow in, *but we're not disturbed by them.* We can see the thoughts that are spam and drag them to the Delete folder, or, even better, put them on silent. Meditation teaches you to proactively choose where to put your energy rather than reactively responding to every blip and beep that comes your way.

But that's only half of the process. With your mind quieted and directed, you can tap into the amazingly clear and peaceful present moment. That's where the bliss is! The present moment is the ticket to everything you're looking for: happiness, love, stability, confidence, wisdom, focus, and deep calm. Once you feel it, you'll want more and more. It's better than vacation. Better than therapy. Better than shopping, or golf, or chocolate. Oh, and it's free!

This is the basic formula that I call "The Simple Formula for Straight-Up Meditation" that brings you there. There are many different ways of meditating, which you'll read about later; this is the simplest and most basic and is ideal for beginners and modern minimalists. On page 136, I'll give you all the details you'll need to be able to do this on your own, but for now, here's a sneak peek at how it works:

You begin by focusing on a single point, like your breath, an object, or a word (a *mantra* — more about mantras later on). This redirects you from your thoughts and shifts you from overdrive into cruise mode. You sit, just breathing and focusing. Nothing fancy, nothing complicated.

At some point, you let go of that focus. It can happen unconsciously, as it usually does in the beginning, or consciously, as you become more aware of this happening; but either way, it's just what your brain does. In that split second of letting go, a gap opens up. For a moment — however brief — you get to drift in that sweet gap of nothingness that is pure awareness. That, right there, is the experience of being fully in the present moment. Not replaying the past or projecting into the future — just being in the here and now.

In the gap is where the good stuff is. It's like *ahhhh* . . . the best gift, the perfect moment of complete awareness, peace, and relaxation. All the stress and noise fall away and you completely appreciate the beauty, the silence, everything. I imagine it like that moment on vacation when I'm fully unwound. I'm lying by the ocean, my book is down, I'm not sleeping or thinking anything other than *This feels good.* That's what the gap feels like. Your time in the gap may last only a millisecond at first, but over time it gets longer and longer and better and better.

The rest of the practice kind of goes in a loop. As soon as you notice your thoughts have crept back in to pull you out of the gap, you acknowledge what's there, refocus on your singular point and start again. That's all there is to it:

Focus.
Let go.
Drift in the gap.
Notice and acknowledge the thoughts resurfacing.
Refocus.
Repeat.

If you think about it, everything is applicable to that formula of coming back to center. And by *center* I mean the here and now in body, mind, and soul. When you're not rehashing the past or worrying about the future, you can think clearly and respond calmly because you're grounded in the present moment. Let's say you mess up and hit Reply All on an e-mail and hurt someone's feelings. Sickening feeling, isn't it? With the practice of meditation grooved into your brain, though, instead of losing hours or days beating yourself up over this mistake that happened in the past, albeit two minutes ago, or worrying about the impact it will have in the future, you can acknowledge it, forgive yourself, and come back to this exact present moment. If you need to make it right, you'll do that. But you'll do it from center. You'll be in control, rather than making matters worse by reacting when supercharged emotions are running the show. This is how meditation changes your life.

Experiencing the present moment in meditation trains your brain to stay awake to it throughout the rest of your day. And really, that's the whole point of all of this. So often we're thinking about anything BUT what's actually happening in front of us, and we're missing the moment we're in right now. You're on vacation thinking about work. You're at work thinking about your kids. You're with your kids daydreaming about where you should go on your next vacation. We're so busy trying to get to the next moment that we're missing out on this one.

Being awake means that when you're with your kids, your friends, or your mate, you'll actually be *with* them. When you're at work, your head will be in the game. When the day ends, you can go home with that satisfied feeling of knowing you did good work. When you eat, you'll stop mindlessly shoveling and actually taste your food. It might sound a little hokey, but everything feels more alive to you when you experience it fully in the present moment.

Meditation helps you embrace the present moments so that they — and your life — don't pass you by. In the end, isn't that all that really matters?

MEDITATION:
DEBUNKED, DEMYSTIFIED, AND TOTALLY DOABLE

I'm guessing you've heard all about the benefits of meditation. These days, it seems like everyone from Deepak Chopra to Harvard scientists to *Time* magazine is raving about how it can radically improve your life on every level.

So knowing all this, are you meditating? No judgments here — but I'm guessing the answer is no, for all the same reasons I wasn't. I believed it would take too much time out of my day; that I'd need to "shut off" my brain, which I couldn't do . . . ; or worse, I'd need to sit perfectly still, which I *definitely* couldn't do. Turns out none of these is true. Because meditation had this air of mystery and mysticism to it, I also assumed it was complicated and hard to learn. Again: not true!

To be honest, I also thought meditation was weird. I always thought that meditators were hippies, monks, or gurus you'd find in either metaphysical bookstores or a cave in the Himalayas. I never imagined they were high-level CEOs using meditation as a tool to kill it in business, or famous television news anchors or actors using it to get calm and centered before going on the air, or stay-at-home moms who did it to find peace in the middle of parenting pressures and carpool chaos. There was definitely a disconnect for me.

There are a lot of misconceptions about meditation floating around out there, and I want to set the record straight so you can see how simple, easy, and un-weird it actually is. For the busy skeptic who wants to cut right to the action, you can skip this section and go straight to page 115 for the how-to part. Or, you can read on to discover ten bottom-line facts about meditation that might surprise you.

1. It's Easy to Learn
I think I just proved that to you. Moving on.

2. Anyone Can Do It
Yes, even you. Even if you never pictured yourself doing anything like this; even if you tried it once before and thought it was boring; even if you think you can't turn off your

brain (see page 58 for a happy news flash: you don't have to); even if you're 100 percent convinced you could never, ever sit still.

As I said, I can completely relate to the sitting-still part. Sometimes I still have a hard time with that. The more you do it, though, the easier it gets. I promise. At first, if you have to shift, adjust, sneeze, or scratch an itch while you're meditating, then do it. Who's stopping you? There's no meditation law that says you have to sit frozen like a statue.

If you're worried it will be boring, I'll level with you: When you first start meditating, sometimes it might feel kind of boring, especially if you're doing it at home by yourself. I mean, let's be honest — you're just sitting there. But very soon, you'll start to experience longer and longer times in that blissful gap. You become aware of the way your mind works, and thoughts begin to make it interesting. Suddenly, you'll just *get it:* You can actually control your brain! Then the bigger results start to show up in your life (see "Strange and Wonderful Things That May Happen," page 72), and boring goes right out the window. You've just got to get past that initial hump, and then you will begin to crave it. Like Steve

Ross, the beloved yoga master and Unplug meditation teacher, says, "In the beginning, you've got to have a little faith in the process. Not a lot. But some."

If you think that meditation just "isn't you," you're not alone. I've heard that from so many people. But saying that meditation "just isn't me" is the same as saying that breathing "just isn't me." If you can breathe, you can meditate.

I'm the girl who always said I couldn't meditate. That my mind is too busy. I'm way too fidgety. I can't get comfortable, blah, blah, blah. Heels dug in. Not for me. But my stress level was off the charts, and I realized that if I didn't do something differently, nothing in my life would change. One day, I felt like I was going to implode, so I listened to the advice of my boyfriend, who meditates almost every day, and went to a class at Unplug. Not only did it work — it worked fast! Meditation helped me find the calm confidence I'd been missing. No one was more surprised than I was that it turned into something I look forward to and expect to continue for a long time.

BETH, 29, BUSINESS DEVELOPMENT
DIRECTOR

3. Nothing Happens (Usually)

Meditation teacher Megan Monahan starts off her classes with something that always makes me laugh. She says, "Spoiler alert: nothing is going to happen in this room." It's usually true. A lot of the time, we just focus on our breath and connect with the power of being fully present. There is no big finish line in meditation, no fireworks, no holy grail, no winning. You're not practicing to achieve anything; getting yourself to sit quietly and breathe at least once a day *is* the achievement.

I'm telling you this so you're not sitting there waiting for some big dramatic moment. And so when it doesn't happen you don't think, "I'm doing it wrong," or, "It's not working." There's not a lot of drama that happens in meditation practice.

And sometimes, you will have some "cool meditation-y moments," as we like to say here in California. Those can be anything from seeing flashes of color, like purple circles, or feeling like you're floating, or having big life epiphanies in which genius ideas and insights pop up. (But don't stop meditation to write them down. If they're really that good, they'll stick around afterward.)

Davidji compares meditations to snowflakes, because no two are ever the same.

Once you understand that every sit will be different, you stop looking to duplicate. The cool moments are not something you can have on demand. They're moments that *sometimes* come with being fully present, but no guarantees!

Even if you don't get the cool moments and are just sitting there battling your brain and switching from your thinking mind to your breath over and over, you're still doing something good. You're still passing through the gap. It's not what happens when you're doing it that matters; it's what happens after.

You might not feel it there on the cushion, but you'll have a greater sense of peace, awareness, and calm in the rest of your day. Outside of the room, you'll notice you get less caught up in story and become more aware of how your mind works. It's like, *Oh, I know I do this or that when things don't go right . . . I'm not going to do that right now, though . . . I'm going to focus on my breath instead . . .* You get to be aware of the way you think, and you shift away from the thoughts and resulting reactions that don't serve you, just like you do inside the room. You may not even realize meditation is the reason until you've been doing it for a little while.

Angela, age forty-two, is an event coordinator for a large corporation. Three times a year, she stages a huge conference for more than two thousand employees — and three times a year she would be *frantic* in the week leading up to the event. Her friends and family got to know the routine so well that they called it "hell week." She started meditating regularly, and it wasn't until the day before one of these conferences that she realized the effect the practice was having on her. She hadn't gone berserk at all this go-around! She laughed when she told me, "Don't get me wrong — it wasn't like everything went perfectly. Please. But somehow I was just able to kind of handle it all without going into hyper-stress mode. I'm so surprised — and my friends and family are AMAZED!"

So don't worry if nothing happens while you're meditating. Because whether you know it or not, big things are going on in there. As Unplug teacher Olivia Rosewood says, "Just because meditation is simple and quiet, don't overlook its power and importance and what it can do for your life."

4. Meditation Is Not Weird

Maybe you're into crystals or lighting incense, and there's absolutely nothing wrong with that. Personally, I love crystals and crystal healing meditation. But if sage smoke makes you cough or you feel silly chanting "ohm," that's okay, too, because you don't have to do any of these things to meditate. You don't have to sit with your hands palm-up in your lap with your forefinger and thumb making an O, or study the sacred geometry of healing stones, or build an altar with a framed photo of a guru on it in the corner of your bedroom in order to get the benefits of the practice. You don't even need to be a vegetarian.

Meditation typically has an aura of mystery and mysticism, so I understand why so many people associate it with all things weird. But I can honestly tell you this after taking many, many hours of classes and courses, meditating daily (okay, almost daily) for five years, reading dozens of books, and talking with so many brilliant modern teachers: Meditation is only weird if you make it weird.

In and of itself, there's nothing new agey or woo-woo about sitting and focusing on a single point to direct your attention. Is it a spiritual experience? Absolutely, it can be.

But hiking to the top of a spectacular mountain or eating the world's most delicious peach can be spiritual, too. All that means is that it's something that inspires or elevates you and touches your soul. You don't even have to go on the whole spiritual journey part if you don't want to (though to me, that's the best part); you'll *still* get the benefits of thinking more clearly and feeling calmer and happier. The trick is to always keep it your own journey and make meditation work for you and your own life.

Speaking of spiritual, let's clear up another myth: Meditation isn't religious. It has five-thousand-year-old roots in Taoist China and Buddhist India, and later Buddhist Japan, but meditation isn't directly connected to any specific religion. Christians, Buddhists, Jews, Muslims, Mormons, and anyone else can and does do it; it's an equal-opportunity life changer.

The practice of meditation is different from prayer. I once heard that prayer is when you send your thoughts and energy out and to something; meditation is when you're going within. Religion is usually rooted in belief in a higher spiritual being. To me, meditation is about connecting with your own truth of who you are and your purpose in life. Instead of directing your energy to a higher power for inspiration and guidance, you're getting those answers from within.

5. Meditation Does Not Have to Be Long to Be Effective

"I'd love to meditate, but I just don't have the time."

I can't tell you how many times I've heard that from people. And you know what? They're right. You won't find the time. You have to make the time.

You're always going to feel like you don't have enough time when you don't make time for yourself. But let's be honest: Anyone can find a few minutes in their day to do something important if they're willing. How many times have you suddenly dropped everything when your kid calls from the school nurse's office, or to go to a hot sold-out show someone suddenly has a spare ticket for, or to help a colleague in a crunch? We make time for the things that matter to us.

So how much time, really, do you need to meditate each day? Some schools of thought say forty minutes a day is ideal, twenty minutes in the morning and twenty minutes at night. Some say thirty minutes total. Technically speaking, according to Harvard neuroscientist Sara Lazar, who conducted breakthrough studies on meditation and the brain (more on this on page 72), if you go from never meditating to doing it once a day for twenty-seven minutes for eight weeks, you will physically alter the structure of your brain for the better. To tell you the truth, though, even ten minutes can make a difference. That's not scientifically proven, but I can tell you I feel it, and so can others.

You'll play around with what works best for you, but take the advice of teacher Laurie Cousins, who tells beginning students to start with the maximum amount of time each day that they know they'll be able to stick to. Be realistic; this is about making it work for you and your life. Even if you do just ten minutes a day, you'll get some of the benefits.

The irony is that when we make the time to meditate, we find we actually have *more* time in our day, not less. Or as Arianna Huffington once told us when she spoke at Unplug, you become "time affluent" — filthy rich with time! You'll actually feel like time stretches for you. Ask anyone who meditates regularly and they'll tell you this is true. Jo, age forty, said, "You think you don't have the time to do it . . . that you have too much to do, you're too busy. But the funny thing is that you'll find yourself able to focus better and get more done if you take the time to meditate."

Here's Megan Monahan's insightful explanation on why we "gain time" through meditating:

There are a lot of things that seem more important than sitting down and "doing nothing." People see it as time spent that they don't really have. The reason they feel they don't have time is because they're constantly looking to the past or the future — two places, by the way, that you have no control over. You're wasting your moments worrying about those, and you lose the potent power that you have in this moment. One of the biggest benefits of meditation is that you become more grounded in this present moment. It gives you a more present-minded viewpoint, and all of a sudden you're more focused and feel like you have more time to get things done because you're not constantly jumping out of the moment you're actually in.

Some of the busiest people on the planet meditate: Oprah Winfrey; Kobe Bryant;

Arianna Huffington. They find the time. So can we.

6. Meditation Won't Make You Lose Your Edge

Worried that meditation will turn your brain to mush or turn you into a blissed-out, checked-out hippie? Don't be. While it will take the edge off your stress, it won't take the edge off *you.* It won't make you any less sharp, less focused, less productive, or less anything (other than less stressed, anxious, agitated, or overwhelmed).

In fact, it's just the opposite.

Studies have proven that having a regular meditation practice actually makes us much *more* functional and *more* productive. I've definitely found this to be true for myself. It clears away the mental clutter and makes me more methodical and thoughtful, less chaotic. I used to wake up, jump out of bed, and slam right into my to-do list. I would go through the day charged up and reactive to everything that came my way, then collapse into bed only to wake up and do it all over again.

Now I slow down in the morning and connect with myself in my meditation. Literally, before I even get out of bed, I just lie there and do my fifteen minutes. Afterward

I can pause and map out *What do I want to achieve today?* I'm proactive rather than reactive. I feel like I'm in charge of my time, rather than feeling at the mercy of anything and everything that comes up minute to minute. I get so much more done now because I don't get sucked into worry spirals or go unconscious as to how I spend my time and lose hours doing things that don't serve what I'm trying to do that day (hello, Internet shopping).

I have just as much drive, passion, and energy as I've always had — more, even. I'm so much more at an advantage because I meditate. I did a lot before I opened this studio, but this was a big undertaking. It's a good thing I had that meditation room right there to go into, because there are moments as a business owner that you want to hide in the corner and cry. You never get to turn it off because people need you 24/7. The software system goes down . . . the front desk manager didn't show up with the key and there are twenty-seven people waiting outside . . . your star teacher announces he's going to India for the next three months. It's not like I just automatically say, "Oh, fine, no big deal" when these things happen. But with the gift of perspective, I'm able to handle and move through them in a much better way. I tackle challenges more thoughtfully and effectively rather than wasting my energy on things I can't control.

When I worked in fashion, I was often in panic mode. Now I'm in productive mode. When something goes wrong, I go into problem solving right away. Before, challenges would stress me out. If I couldn't get Michael Kors Look #37 for a photo shoot, I would go crazy until I did. Now, if I can't get Look #37 — or whatever the equivalent is in my new life — I switch gears within moments and know I'm going to find a better one.

I'm still competitive, just in a different way. I don't look to my right and left anymore, because I don't need to. I compete with myself. There's no less fire under me — it's just lit from within instead of trying to outblaze others'. My ideas are clearer than they've ever been before, and I can see the path to make them into reality. A lot of people say trust your gut, but they can't hear it because they're too busy. I can actually hear mine, because I'm clear. That's the competitive advantage, right there. It's like when the Seattle Seahawks won the Super Bowl in 2013 after their head coach, Pete Carroll, brought in famous sports psychologist Michael Gervais to teach them meditation. An ABC News journalist joked that they had the "ohm team advantage."

We have a lot of high-level executives who come to our classes, and they tell us that meditation helps them focus and make logical decisions rather than emotional ones. That's a distinct advantage. If the legendary billionaire hedge fund founder Ray Dalio says, "More than anything in my life, meditation was the biggest ingredient of whatever success I've had," I think we can all agree that meditation doesn't dull any edges.

I am a far better listener and leader to my very diverse team because of the tools I've developed through regular meditation. I used to get very caught up in the frenetic pace of my day, and sometimes paralyzed by the myriad decisions I had to make in the course of a week. I now am able to pull back, be present and thoughtful about next steps, and make far better decisions. I also no longer create narratives around what "might happen" — I focus on where I am, and what I can affect NOW. Shockingly (and hilariously), I am now considered the "level-headed" one! My team has noticed a vast difference in me, and the productivity/engagement of my group is beyond what I could have hoped.

KATHY, 54, VICE PRESIDENT AND
GENERAL MANAGER OF
BLOOMINGDALE'S

7. You Don't Need to "Turn Off" Your Brain

The biggest myth out there about meditation is that we're supposed to clear our minds or stop our thoughts. Which is good news for me, because my brain goes 24/7, probably just like yours.

The object of meditation definitely is not to halt your thoughts — which is impossible, anyway. It's to let them come up, then let them go and come back to your focus point, again and again and again. The process is the practice. It's kind of like mental exercise or a bicep curl. You keep doing the same thing, and eventually, you build up strength. Then, when you're out in your everyday life, that mental muscle is ready to work for you. Very soon, you notice that it takes you less time to catch yourself "drifting off," and you're able to bring yourself back sooner.

I'll show you how this plays out in your daily life. The other day, I went out to the parking lot to get my car to drive to a meeting and discovered someone had blocked me in. Our studio is in a building with a lot of psychiatrists' offices, and it was ten minutes past the hour, so my immediate reaction was *Who does this? What an idiot! I have a meeting . . . OMG. This is going to take an hour. I'm stuck in here.* I started off reactive, literally feeling myself heating up.

It's not as if I don't get irritated like that anymore. Remember, *you can't stop thoughts and feelings from coming up.* The difference is that now, I can quickly redirect them so the irritation doesn't take over. So after a few seconds, I stopped, took a breath, and realized I could get all crazy, but it wouldn't do much. So I just accepted it and was about to go back inside to make a new travel plan.

Then something happened I didn't expect. The woman came out of the building to move her car, realizing she might be blocking someone in. I'll be honest: In the past, I might have driven off in a huff, letting her know how annoyed I was — which would have had an impact on her, and then later made me feel bad for being rude. I could have lost ten minutes of my life just being angry and feeling tensed up and gotten really mad at her and at myself. But instead,

I only felt the negativity for a moment and was able to quickly unhook from it and respond in a kinder, more rational way. I actually thanked her for thinking of it and not making me wait until her appointment was over. That's the meditation in me at work.

It's important to let your emotions pop up so you can let them go and move on. Suppressed emotions cause illness and depression, and who wants that? Meditating doesn't stop you from feeling any more than it stops you from thinking — it just lets you become aware of your emotions and thoughts sooner. Once you become aware of a feeling that's taking over, you can step back and observe it. You realize your thoughts and emotions are not you — they're separate. You are not sad; you *feel* sad. You are not angry; you *feel* angry. Separating *you* from *how you're feeling* is the way to freedom — the direct path back to your calm, rational mind.

Trying to stop or push negative thoughts away doesn't work. The trick is to actually let them come in, and notice and fully experience them so you can then let them go. A little later I'll give you all the insider tips and tricks to be able to "let go" of the thoughts that are bringing you down or riling you up. It's a lot easier than you think.

I have gone to workshops and purchased CDs but I never really felt as though I could actually meditate until a few things clicked for me. First, when I learned the idea that you don't stop your thoughts. That's such a popular myth! Then, the concept that you can see yourself as merely the thinker of the thoughts, and that they are always coming and going but you can recenter by simply going back to the breath (or the mantra). Huge! These two subtle shifts in thinking really opened my eyes — and my mind.

LANA, 43, PUBLIC RELATIONS
EXECUTIVE

8. There Is No Such Thing as a Bad Meditation

The only bad meditation is the one you don't do.

That's what Davidji says, and I agree. Every meditation practice is valuable — even the challenging ones. There are definitely frustrating meditation sessions when you find yourself battling with your brain, but those are actually the *most* valuable. The more you battle, the stronger your redirect muscle becomes. Sometimes redirecting your focus will come easily, sometimes not, but either way, you're building the muscle and literally growing your brain (more about this soon).

I still have meditations that feel frustrating. This usually happens when I'm meditating inside the studio instead of at home. I'm the owner of the business, so my natural inclination is to care deeply about the experience everyone else in the room is having. I want them to love it! So I'm mentally scanning the room for ways it could be better for them. But if I'm truly there to meditate, I have to stop the "We need to fix this or improve that" and redirect to my focus right here and now. I have to let go of the idea that I need to regulate the environment and just be okay with the way things are in this minute (the funny part is that when I do this, I can tune in, and much bigger and better ideas come through). That's the beginning of what I call bliss: being totally present and letting go of the idea that I can control the circumstances. It's amazing how much happier that makes me.

Some meditations, I only get thirty seconds of peace. But even though I may label that as a "bad meditation," it's not, because I'm still conditioning my brain. It's brain training. The meditation teacher and author Light Watkins calls the repeated exercise of going from thoughts to focus "inner jumping jacks." Yoga master Baron Baptiste calls it "fitness for your inner witness." Whatever you want to call building that mental muscle, it's all good for you.

Now and then, I still find myself floating in and out of sessions, my thoughts scrambling to take control. Here's what's different: I used to get disappointed in myself for feeling like I flubbed the session. Now, I've learned to accept my non-acceptance. Ha. The irony, right? I just breathe and smile inside and keep on breathing, self-judgment and all.
  CJ, 57, AUTHOR AND BOOK EDITOR

9. There Are as Many Ways to Meditate as There Are to Make an Egg

This is a quote from meditation teacher Olivia Rosewood, who is one of the most joyful, sparkly, loving people you'll ever meet. Olivia learned to meditate at the age of eighteen from George Harrison (yes, *that* George Harrison) and spent years traveling around the world working directly with Eckhart Tolle — and that only scratches the surface of how cool and knowledgeable she is. Actually, her exact quote — which I've adopted because I agree 100 percent — is "There are as many ways to meditate as there are to make an egg . . . and I love them all!"

When you first venture into the world of meditation, you're bombarded with all these different styles. It's as overwhelming as the cereal aisle at the supermarket. Everyone says it's either their way or the highway, as if the other brands are not as good, but I don't agree. When I first started exploring all this, I made a commitment to be open minded, and what I found is that even though the styles all had different labels, they all shared some basic principles. Just like cereal, some are better for you than others, and some you might like more. But whether you love Raisin Bran or Chex, underneath it all, you're still eating cereal.

There are lots of lineages in the world of meditation, and you could spend years studying the history and the ins and outs of each type. It's interesting to learn, but honestly, you don't *need* this information in order to meditate. I'll give you a quick cheat sheet here so you can see how they're all connected but also different. Once you get going, I encourage you to try out any and all of these styles, to see what works best for you.

There are three main camps of meditation:

1. Camp Mantra
2. Camp Mindful
3. Camp Guided Awareness

In Camp Mantra, you have what's called "mantra-based meditation." *Mantra* is a Sanskrit word that translates to "mind instrument": *ma* for mind and *tra* for instrument. A mantra is a word that you repeat over and over silently to yourself as your point of focus. It's a meaningless word that moves you away from your inner chatter and into yourself. It's usually something very simple, like *ohm* or *I am.* You let in all sounds and sensations around you, but when you notice your mind has wandered off from your mantra, you gently and kindly bring yourself back to it.

That's the practice; you begin over and over. Occasionally (and with increasing frequency, the more you do it), you experience the gap between focus on the mantra and normal thoughts. That's the space of nothingness without worry, fear, or distraction. It's a beautiful feeling of spaciousness and pure awareness. And then . . . BAM!

Your mind sucks you out of that beautiful space and back into thoughts. The way back again is through your mantra.

I like using a mantra because it's a quick, easy tool to move away from thoughts. It's kind of like counting; you can't count from one to ten and think at the same time. Try it right now and you'll see what I mean.

On the grounds of Camp Mantra are three different bunks:

Bunk One: Transcendental Meditation ("TM")
Bunk Two: Vedic Meditation
Bunk Three: Primordial Sound

TM is the style of meditation started by the Maharishi Mahesh Yogi, famously known as the Beatles' guru. He developed TM in India and brought it to the West in the late 1950s. TM has its own trademarked mantras that are energetically charged by the Maharishi, which they give to you as your own secret word that you're not supposed to reveal to anyone else. You work one-on-one with an instructor for four days, usually in their home or a meditation center. The teaching begins with a special ceremony, in which you give him or her flowers and fruit, and they sing a Sanskrit song and light incense on an altar that is covered in rice, mala beads (Hindu prayer beads), and a framed picture of the Maharishi Mahesh Yogi. They teach you about the philosophy of meditation and you meditate with them each time for twenty minutes, using this personal word to move away from your thinking mind and into your quiet center of here and now. This is the short version of what TM is; you can read about it more in depth at the official TM website, tm.org.

Next door, in Bunk Two, you've got Vedic Meditation. Vedic came before Transcendental Meditation and is similar, only without a trademark. Vedic mantras have been handed down by many different gurus. Though the altar and ceremony look similar to the ones used in TM, the guru in the frame is not consistently the same.

Keep on down the path and you come to Bunk Three: Primordial Sound. This style of meditation uses a mantra that creates a specific vibrational sound. For instance, "ohm." Primordial Sound is deeply rooted in the Vedic tradition. They believe there is a particular sound that resonates with you based on the sound the universe was making the moment you were born. There are teachers who can calculate for you your own primordial sound or, if you just want to try this out on your own, you can just repeat "ohm" deeply so it resonates in your chest, and see how it feels.

Across the lake you have Camp Mindful. The campers over here think they're very different from the ones at Camp Mantra, but in essence, the experience is similar, minus the ceremony. Instead of using a mantra, however, you use your breath to take you to the same place. You can also use an external focal point, like a candle flame, a scent, a taste — anything that anchors you to the present moment. Scientific evidence shows that your brain indicates similar effects and results whether you focus on your breath, a sensation, or a word. Remember, it's all cereal, and it's all good.

Jon Kabat-Zinn and Jack Kornfield are the founders of Camp Mindful. Jon Kabat-Zinn is the author of the meditation classic *Wherever You Go, There You Are* and the founder of the famous Mindfulness-Based Stress Reduction (MBSR) program, an eight-week course originally developed in 1979 at the University of Massachusetts Medical Center. The benefits of MBSR have been scientifically proven to help people cope with everything from everyday stress to life-threatening illnesses. Hundreds of medical centers around the world, including Duke Integrative Medicine and the MD Anderson Cancer Center, offer programs modeled on this course.

Jack Kornfield is widely considered one of the founding fathers of Buddhism in the West. He's a bestselling author who has been teaching meditation for more than forty years. Kornfield pioneered the practice of Vipassana, a Buddhist version of mindfulness meditation that originated in India (the Sanskrit word *vipassana* means "to see things as they really are"). Still breath, still singular focus, just a different name and a different intellectual and spiritual basis.

Finally, down the road, you have the third camp, Camp Guided Awareness. At Camp Guided Awareness, your guide leads you on a journey to a specific place through his or her verbal instructions. I like to think of Camp Guided Awareness as a cool space camp, because it's kind of like going on a flight to new places. Think traveling to the Caribbean in your mind, or visiting your future self, or uncovering hidden desires or dreams you never knew you had. I love guided imagery because I never know what I'm going to experience or discover.

In guided imagery, instead of focusing on a mantra or on your breath, you focus on the instructor's voice and follow the imagined path they are leading you on. You drift off into thoughts and, instead of bringing your focus back to a mantra or your breath, you redirect to the guide's voice and your imagination.

So, all this is to say: Scrambled, poached, or sunny side up . . . it's worth it to try every style to see which you like best!

Speaking of the many different ways to meditate . . .

10. Running/Cooking/Playing Golf Isn't Meditation

A lot of people think of running, or driving, or reading, or whatever else they do consistently to "get in the zone" as their meditation. Yes, these kinds of activities are *meditative,* in that they can get you out of your normal thought stream. But they aren't *meditation.* You're unplugging in a way that definitely has value, but there's one crucial difference. With these activities, you're drifting, which is the exact opposite of focusing your attention on a single point. As you now know, that focus is the whole point of meditation. The redirecting of your attention when it wanders is the act that over time reshapes your brain — and your life.

As Davidji explains, "If you're just allowing the thoughts to flow in and out, you'll

70

be taken on this giant journey that really amounts to a lot of daydreaming. But if you have an object of your attention to come back to, like your breath, then you're cultivating something."

So by all means go for a run, or whip up a batch of cookies if it relaxes you. And then sit down to meditate so you can ultimately enjoy and appreciate these things a hundred times more than you already do.

STRANGE AND WONDERFUL
THINGS THAT MAY HAPPEN

I genuinely want everyone on the planet to meditate. That's my goal, because it makes *everyone* better. I know this is true because of what I've seen and experienced, but even better, like I said before, there is serious science to back up almost every claim you've heard about the powers of meditation.

There are so many reasons to meditate, but I think the most compelling one is that it *literally* changes your brain. It physically alters the shape of your gray matter to make you smarter, happier, and calmer. This isn't just hype; it's been scientifically proven.

Sara Lazar is a neuroscientist at Massachusetts General Hospital and Harvard Medical School who did two separate studies that showed — in actual brain images — how meditation reshapes the brain. She summed it all up in a fascinating TEDx talk, which is really worth watching, but I'll give you the high points here:

First, she compared the brain scans of people from the Boston area who meditated regularly versus those of people who didn't. In the regular meditators, she found several regions in the brain that had more gray matter — primarily the frontal cortex, which is the part that controls memory and executive decision making. It's been well documented that this part shrinks as we get older; that's why we routinely can't seem to find our glasses and take longer to make choices. But — and here's where this gets really cool — the scans showed that fifty-year-old meditators had as much gray matter in that region as twenty-five-year-old non-meditators. In other words: no shrinking, no memory fuzziness, no slowing of thought processes.

But was this because they had been meditating for so long? Sara Lazar wanted to find out, so she and her colleagues did a second study on people who had never meditated. They scanned their brains and then had one group do the eight-week MBSR course, in which they were asked to meditate daily for thirty to forty minutes (the average was twenty-seven minutes per day). At the end of the eight weeks, when Lazar rescanned their brains and compared the scans of the new meditators with those of the non-meditators, the results were still astonishing. She saw marked physical changes in the brain regions that control learning, memory, focus, emotional regulation, empathy, and more.

That's one of the biggest reasons why I love meditation. You don't have to try. You just have to sit and *do it,* and your brain gets rewired.

Then there are all the other life-changing benefits of meditation. Everyone's meditation results are different, but I have yet to meet anyone who hasn't experienced at least some of these positive changes. Here's my sizzle reel of favorites, complete with some of my favorite insights from meditation experts:

You'll Be Happier

Meditation is an essential tool in getting the most joy out of life.

OLIVIA ROSEWOOD

One of my favorite things to do is watch students' faces go from stressed to serene, right there during their meditation. They rush into the studio straight from Los Angeles traffic hell, looking hassled and harried, and practically glide out of the meditation room forty-five minutes later looking as if they just spent a week at a spa.

But it's what happens to them over a few weeks — or for some, even a few days — that really gets me. People are just *happier.* They're sunnier and lighter. They stand up straighter. They smile more. The increase in joy is tangible in how they look, how they sound, how they walk, and how they interact with people around them.

This hit of happiness is real. Even better, it lasts, because we're reconfiguring our capacity for happiness by rewiring our brains. Little happiness boosters like vacations are nice, but they've got no staying power. Researchers in the Netherlands discovered that the effects of a "very relaxing" vacation wear off after just two weeks. Meditation is so much cheaper than flying off to a beach somewhere, and there are many scientific studies showing it makes us happier in the long term. You get to keep the glow going for as long as you want.

We all have what psychologists call our "happiness set point," which is our individual capacity for joy. Mine might be high, someone else's might be low. But the good news for those who weren't born naturally happy is that this set point *is not carved in stone.* It's been proven that we can grow new neurons, which means we can train our brains to go from mildly happy to wildly happy. Or, as meditation teacher Amy Budden likes to say, "Meditation can trump environment and genes to help you hardwire happiness." So there literally is no cap on the amount of happiness you can experience!

Here are just a few of the studies out there that prove meditation makes us happier:

- Neuroscientist Sara Lazar's studies showed that meditation shrinks the amygdala, the part of the brain that controls anxiety and fear. Less anxiety and fear translates to less stress. Less stress means more joy.
- A study done by research scientists at UC Davis showed that meditation can lower the amount of cortisol in the body, otherwise known as the stress hormone. Less cortisol, less stress, more capacity for joy. Seeing the pattern here?
- Richard Davidson, PhD, and his colleagues at the University of Wisconsin, along with Jon Kabat-Zinn, put group of stressed biotech employees through Kabat-Zinn's eight-week MBSR program (if you need a quick refresher on

this, see page 68). They found that the employees who completed the program had more activity in the left prefrontal cortex — the happy, calm zone of the brain — than those who didn't do the training.

- A study done by Yale researchers showed that experienced meditators are able to dial down their daydreaming. Why does this matter? Because when our minds meander, they usually drift into worry or rumination, so less mind wandering is associated with more happiness. According to a different study done at Harvard, people reported being much less happy when their minds were wandering than when they were fully engaged in whatever they were doing. Being present, it turns out, is a ticket to being happy.
- A study done at the Johns Hopkins University School of Medicine and published in *JAMA Internal Medicine* showed that meditation can provide a level of relief from symptoms of anxiety and depression similar to that of anti-depressant drugs. Peace and happiness, no prescription needed!

When I first started meditating, I was in

a really icky place. I was going through a divorce and had gotten my heart broken in my rebound relationship. I was so sad and lonely because I'd been in a relationship my entire adult life. I committed to meditation and practiced it three times a week for a full month, and session after session, I started to notice changes.

The first thing I noticed was that my sad feelings were lessening and I was becoming more okay with being on my own. I was feeling happier, more adventurous, and open to new things. Overall, I just felt more balanced and calm; things like traffic or criticism didn't bother me as much. And now that I'm back in the dating world again, I'm able to realize what's a good situation for me and what isn't. I don't overanalyze or take things so personally anymore. I feel grateful for everything I have and for everything around me. I'm just much more present and in the moment. I could go on and on, because meditation has completely changed my life for the better in so many ways! Give it a month and just do it, and see what happens.

COURTNEY, 35, TELEVISION NEWS
REPORTER

You'll Be Better Able to Handle Life's Challenges

Meditation creates resilience, and resilience is paramount to having a happy life, because you're able to bounce back and go with the flow. That doesn't mean you won't have challenges — just that you'll have the tools to be able to work with them as opposed to feeling overwhelmed or victimized by them. You learn that you have choice in how you respond.

LAURIE COUSINS

Something irritating happens. You react.

Something disappointing happens. You react again.

A third, fourth, fifth thing happens. React, react, react.

This is how most of us go through our days. It's completely normal, and totally automatic: Something crosses our path that's unexpected and we have an instantaneous knee-jerk reaction to it. There's no pause in between the stimulus and the response. It just goes:

EVENT → AUTOMATIC RESPONSE

The problem is that a lot of the time, what gets triggered is negative. We hit a challenge

79

and immediately feel angry, anxious, frustrated, guilty, and so forth. This kind of automatic response doesn't just feel bad; it clouds our ability to think rationally and clearly and to respond thoughtfully, so it keeps us stuck in the muck even longer.

Meditation frees us from that by creating a little gap between the event and your response. It's like hitting an imaginary Pause button that freezes time and lets you calm and collect yourself, all within a split second.

Let's say your computer freezes at the worst possible moment. Big deadline looming . . . it's not good. Your usual options might be to go into:

a. Sputtering panic
b. Ranting fury at the manufacturer or technology in general
c. Self-flagellation that you ignored the flashing "critical update required" notice that kept popping up

Or you could hit the Pause button in between the moment the screen goes haywire and your automatic reaction. In this scenario, the event occurs, the automatic response kicks in, except — and here's where the big change happens — you *notice* the response kick in. The instant you notice it, you separate from it. In that tiny gap that opens up, you get to *choose* how you want to respond. You get to respond consciously rather than zooming straight into ramped-up autopilot mode. So instead of: EVENT → AUTOMATIC RESPONSE, it looks more like this:

EVENT → BREATHE, PAUSE, THINK →
RESPOND CALMLY AND
CONSCIOUSLY

The beauty of meditation is that the rewiring happens all by itself after you've been practicing for a little while. You don't have to do anything but practice. Observing your thoughts during meditation practice trains your mind to separate from them, and the separation gives you back your power of choice.

Here's a great trick I learned from Unplug teacher Natalie Bell to help separate you from your thoughts and emotions. Natalie works with many executives and corporations, including the National Football League, Chipotle, Deutsche Bank, the Wharton School of Business, and others, so she's well versed in how valuable it is to be able to unhook from faulty automatic wiring and respond from a calm, rational place. When the thoughts or feelings come up, you label them. For instance, *Oh, I'm getting angry* or *I'm nervous.* It sounds simplistic, but it's really powerful. As Natalie explains, science shows us that when we label the thought behind a feeling, the amygdala (the fight-or-flight part of your brain that generates stress) begins to calm down. This is the way in which you become the observer of the thought, and not overly tangled up in it. If you see the thought, then it's separate from you; you're over here, and the thought is over there. It lets you step outside of it, observe it, and then let it go so you can come back to the here and now, center, the zone . . . whatever you want to call it.

Labeling is a helpful tool, especially when you first start meditating. I still use it. As soon as I notice I've drifted off, I label what's happening, and that directs me back to my breath. Sometimes it might be *I'm making to-do lists in my head again;* other times it could be *I'm frustrated that I can't relax.* Then I direct my attention back to my breath, and I can easily let go of the inner chatter. Over time, you'll start to do this process of labeling and letting go naturally without having to go through the whole cognitive cycle.

One caveat from Natalie on this whole idea of "letting go" is that we shouldn't confuse *letting go* of thoughts and feelings with pushing them away. They're not the same. Pushing away your thoughts and emotions doesn't ever really work, anyway, because they always come back. What we're really doing is "letting be." We allow the thoughts to come up and become aware of them so we can then notice and let them go and not get trapped in our reaction to them. Any and all thoughts that come up should be welcomed, because that means they're no longer secretly controlling you.

Eventually, as you keep conditioning your brain, something even more remarkable happens. Life's little challenges won't seem so challenging because you can actually shift the way you think about them. You start to build up your resilience and your ability to be with what's here in the moment. You let go of the internal struggle of wishing things were different from exactly how they are, and instead you can handle whatever comes up from a calm center and with clear eyes. It doesn't mean you won't care when life throws you a curveball — it just means you'll stay in the zone that allows you to field it with calm precision. The more you do this, the more your overall outlook on life changes.

Meditation also helps us through the big stuff in life — pretty profoundly. You may not even realize the effect your practice is having on you until you hit a serious challenge and suddenly see how much better equipped you are to deal with it. Olivia Rosewood went through the heartbreaking experience of having two daughters born with birth defects. Both needed multiple surgeries for survival that put them in and out of the hospital for several years. During one of these surgeries, her younger daughter was deprived of oxygen and left with permanent brain damage. Hearing all of this, you might expect Olivia to be angry or bitter, but she is the polar opposite. She says, "I feel so lucky and grateful that I get to have this challenge of having a special needs child, because it deepens me. I think this is what all my meditative practice and training was for. When you're faced with big challenges like life-or-death situations, your meditation past can be an energetic savings account for you to draw on. It allows you to accept what is, rather than resisting it."

Amazing, isn't she?

That level of positivity and resilience is truly what meditation can do for us if we just sit down, close our eyes, and breathe with intention on a daily basis.

After going through a bunch of major changes in my life — getting married, changing careers, having a kid — all within two years, I started getting panic attacks. My heart would race out of control. I actually went to the hospital twice, thinking I was having a heart attack. The emergency room attendants would roll their eyes and suggest I go take Xanax, but to me, it made more sense to try something other than drugs to calm down. So I started meditating, and it changed everything.

I guess the best way to put it is that meditation allowed me to sit on a park bench, so to speak, and just watch things go by in my mind. It allowed me to take control of pretty much anything I was feeling by grounding myself. No matter where I was, I would close my eyes and allow my breath to anchor me, like that park bench. Everything else — the anxious feeling, for instance — I would give a label to and allow myself to simply observe it, rather than experiencing it.

To me, meditation is a way of knowing how to live peacefully right in the middle of stress. You can't change many of the things that go on around you, so it makes a lot more sense to try to live with them in harmony. Meditation doesn't tell you how to ignore the noise, but how to live with it. We never stop hearing the noise. Part of successful meditation is the acceptance of that and not thinking the stress goes away — it just gets managed better.

PAUL, 46, TRADER

You'll Be More Successful

Meditation gives you the clarity and focus to perform at your best. As you train the CEO of your brain, decisions get clearer and your work becomes more productive and fulfilling.

NATALIE BELL

Ask anyone who meditates regularly and they'll tell you this is true. Why? Because your focus will improve, your memory will be sharper, and you'll be able to steer yourself — at will — to the part of your brain that gets sh-t done. Plus, as I heard media mogul Russell Simmons, who is a dedicated meditator, say at the Milken Institute 2016 Global Conference, "Meditation makes you happy, and happy makes you money."

Teacher Lena George is a self-described "brain nerd." A certified hypnotherapist and Advanced EFT (Emotional Freedom Technique)/tapping practitioner (more about that on page 197), she's a go-to expert on the neurological effects of meditation. Here's her download on how meditation makes us more productive:

Meditation helps us think more rationally. We train our brain to switch from one part of our brain (the amygdala, which is the primitive, reactive part) to the other (the prefrontal cortex, which controls higher thinking). Stress is really about feeling threatened. When we feel threatened, we go into the primitive brain and respond by either fighting or fleeing.

When we're in a stressed state, we're usually all over the place — in other words, unfocused and unproductive. We're functioning from a reactive place, not a rational and proactive one. Meditation allows us to switch out of that fight/flight brain and into our calmer, more rational mind, otherwise known as the prefrontal cortex. That's the part that controls big-picture thinking and executive decision making. You can escape the limited thinking that keeps you trapped in panic and step into effective problem-solving mode.

Need more proof that meditation will sharpen your skills for success? Here you go:

- Did you know that studies show multitasking can cut our efficiency as much as 40 percent? Meditation teaches us to become more singularly focused, which automatically allows us to become more efficient.
- Corporate culture has caught on in a big way. Some of the most successful companies in the world — including Apple, Google, Nike, Procter & Gamble, General Mills, Aetna, and Deutsche Bank — offer meditation classes for their employees. Some even have dedicated meditation rooms on-site.
- Meditation training translates to dollars. Studies done by eMindful, a provider of online mindfulness-based programs for employers, showed that after five years, companies saw a return of nearly ten dollars for every dollar they invested in the program. Just know that meditation by itself won't make you richer. It will definitely clear

away the mental clutter and make you sharper, more focused, more creative, and more productive, but the rest is on you!

- Studies prove that meditation training can improve students' test scores.
- If you're a creative type, meditation is better than any muse. You'll rewire your brain so you can more easily shift out of the amygdala and into the prefrontal cortex, where the inspiration turns into brilliant ideas, and ideas into execution. We have so many writers and artists at our studio who tell me that they came up with their big idea while meditating with us that I started to joke we should get a commission!

By the way, all these stats on success aren't just for business types. Meditation can make *anyone* more successful in whatever they do. Athletes — including, most famously, Kobe Bryant, Derek Jeter, and Super Bowl winners the Seattle Seahawks — use it to boost their performance and focus. Artists, writers, and musicians say it makes their creativity flow better. Busy parents find they can juggle their priorities better to spend more quality time with their kids. One of our students is a life coach and teacher who said meditation has allowed him to support his clients on a deeper level. Productivity value isn't always about dollars.

If I could go back and say only one thing to my twenty-year-old self it would be this: Go learn to pay attention to your breath and meditate. It will make all the difference. After only about a year of regularly taking a few minutes each day to be present and invest in myself, I have found greater calm, focus, and efficiency across every area of my life — more vibrant moments with family, increased calm and purpose at work, and a truer, stronger belief in myself.

CLINT, 40, PRESIDENT OF
MADISON WELLS MEDIA

You'll Be Healthier
Here's what we know:

Stress makes us sick. It's been estimated that up to 95 percent of all illnesses are caused or made worse by stress. Ouch.
Meditation is proven to reduce stress.
Conclusion: A meditation a day keeps the doctor away!

Here's how and why you'll be significantly healthier if you meditate.

Your Immunity May Improve

Remember that study that Richard Davidson and Jon Kabat-Zinn did with stressed biotech employees? One group did the eight-week Mindfulness-Based Stress Reduction program; the other didn't. The researchers gave both groups a flu vaccine at the end of the eight weeks and found that the meditators produced many more antibodies. More antibodies = less flu.

You'll Age More Slowly

I *love* this one. In 2009, Elizabeth Blackburn along with Carol Greider and Jack Szostak won the Nobel Prize for their work surrounding *telomeres,* which are the protective structures at the end of our chromosomes (imagine plastic shoelace caps). When our cells divide, these telomeres shorten and fray — not a good thing: Shortened telomeres are associated with aging and cancer. But in 2012, Blackburn and scientists at UCLA found that as little as twelve minutes a day of meditation for eight weeks could increase telomerase activity (the "immortality enzyme" that repairs telomeres) by 43 percent. In other words, meditation can repair our DNA and slow the aging process. Pretty compelling stuff, no?

Your Heart Will Be Protected

We get a lot of people sent to us from UCLA Medical Center on the advice of their doctors, so to find out more about why meditation is good for your heart, I talked with Dr. Tamara Beth Horwich, associate professor of Medicine/Cardiology at UCLA, codirector of the UCLA Women's Cardiovascular Center, and medical director of the UCLA Cardiac Rehabilitation Program. Here's what she had to say:

> We're learning more and more that stress is a major risk factor for heart disease. Just a few months ago, I had a patient come in who was model gorgeous — a vegan who hikes and bikes, with no high blood pressure or high cholesterol. She appeared to be in great shape. Yet the one thing in her life that wasn't on track was her high stress. She came in with a heart attack, and when we looked at her profile, the only thing we could pinpoint was that she wasn't managing her stress.
>
> There is a lot of evidence suggesting that meditation can prevent heart disease.

It can lower blood pressure, lower blood sugar levels, lower stress hormones — all risk factors for cardiovascular disease. At UCLA, we have an intensive cardiac rehabilitation program, and a big piece of it is meditation. Meditation in and of itself helps manage stress, but it also helps people adhere to a whole healthy lifestyle program.

Your Blood Pressure May Lower

Researchers at the Benson-Henry Institute for Mind Body Medicine at Massachusetts General Hospital found that two-thirds of subjects trained in meditation lowered their blood pressure. One of our students was shocked to find out that her blood pressure — which had been borderline high to high her whole adult life, between 135 to 148 mm Hg systolic and 90 to 95 mm Hg diastolic — dropped down dramatically to 106/76 without any lifestyle changes other than meditating thirty minutes a day four to five times a week!

You'll Be Less Sensitive to Pain

When we go into meditation, we release up to 65 percent more dopamine (the feel-good hormone), as well as endorphins; together, those help numb pain. Meditation teacher

Kristen Luman, a hypnotherapist specializing in pain management, explains that there's also a mental aspect to pain control: Something can click in the brain that allows us to control pain rather than having it control us.

I want to tell you about Alan, age thirty-eight, who came to Unplug on crutches after being diagnosed with a rare and debilitating neurological pain disorder in his ankle. Worse, there is no known cure. For someone who was an athlete and soon-to-be new dad, this news was as bad as he could imagine. At the advice of a specialist, he began a mind-body treatment plan that included daily meditation. Within a few months, he was pretty much back to his old life. Here's how Alan describes his experience:

In the course of my healing, I noticed that the meditation gave me a respite from the constant pain. Even if I got a ten-minute break from the pain, it was hugely positive, because I was able to see glimpses of getting my life back. I could use it as hope I would get better. Outside of the pain, it helped me deal with the stress of this issue and redirecting the thoughts of *OMG, what's going to happen to my life?*

One thing my doctor said was that catastrophizing my issue was causing more stress, which then sent more pain signals. Meditation helped me break that catastrophic loop and see that it was all going to be fine.

You'll Release Tension from Your Body
You know that incredible feeling you get when you walk out of a massage, or even a really good workout or yoga session, after all the tension and stress have been pummeled and kneaded out of your muscles? You can save yourself the hefty price tag, because meditation has the same effect! I've seen it happen hundreds of times at this point, where meditators' stress-induced aches, pains, and other symptoms all but disappear.

You'll Sleep Better
Let's face it, when you don't sleep, you look and feel crappy. Under-eye circles and brain fog aren't pretty, but lack of sleep also compromises your immunity (hello, colds and flu) and puts you at risk for long-term diseases ranging from depression to diabetes. Several studies have proven that meditation significantly helps you get better zzz's, and dozens of former insomniacs I've met

attest to that. One told me it used to take her up to four hours every night to fall asleep, and now she can doze off in ten minutes. Another swears by it as her middle-of-the-night insomnia remedy. Her exact words were "It's like natural Xanax. You don't need that stuff when you have meditation."

I woke up one morning with chest pains. Thankfully, it wasn't a heart attack. It was just as scary, however, as this condition mimics a heart attack. It was caused by relentless stress and anxiety. My public relations business was booming, but my personal balance was suffering. This was a giant wake-up call. I immediately realized it was time for some changes. Meditating was one of the most important things I did for myself at that time and it carries through with me today.

Thanks to meditation, I am more present, peaceful, and centered. It helps me not to "go down the rabbit hole" of worrying about what's about to happen or ruminating on past challenges. I have post-traumatic stress disorder, so this is a tremendous gift. I also enjoy deeper, more restful sleep. I never thought it was possible to feel this clear and calm. I have always been a detail-oriented person, but now I really notice the hummingbirds, butterflies, or a gentle breeze. I think that I savor these things so much more after incorporating a meditation practice.

LANA, 43,
PUBLIC RELATIONS EXECUTIVE

You'll Need Less and Less *Stuff* to Fulfill You

Meditation allows us to gain intimacy with ourselves and to realize — truly realize — that we have everything we need inside of us.

DANIELLE BEINSTEIN

Shortly after I moved to Los Angeles, I went to a party at the Museum of Contemporary Art featuring the performance artist Marina Abramović. A group of her people were dressed in white lab coats, holding white coffee cups with holes in them. They mingled with the crowd chanting over and over, "An artist wants more and more of less and less."

This was exactly what I needed to hear at that moment. I realized that I myself wanted

97

more and more of less and less. This was a big revelation to me. Remember, I'm a former fashion editor who spent a lot of years surrounded by stuff. Lots of it — the more, the better! I loved to shop and wanted everything I saw. Beautiful shoes, clothes, and accessories were my weakness, but it didn't really end there. I was the ultimate impulse buyer. Big-box bulk stores were a minefield of everything I never knew I wanted. I would go with the intention of buying groceries and come home with LED candles, polar fleece booties, and a dozen other random stupid things I didn't need. But suddenly, when I heard that sentence, I realized that the more stuff we pile on, the less clarity we have. It was time to clean house, so to speak, to get to higher, clearer ground.

We live in a society that thinks getting something or somewhere will make us happy. On some level, we know that expensive shoes and mansions won't make us happy. They may be fun to have, but they don't equal happiness. So what does?

What makes you happy is knowing what truly makes you happy and what doesn't. That's the secret: knowing your own mind. When you're just going through the motions and acquiring or achieving, you're not stopping and questioning what genuinely fulfills you down in your soul. So you just keep chasing after more stuff, always feeling like something is missing.

For a long time, I just kept buying and buying, and the happiness hit would fade within days or even hours. Now I get that "more" isn't the goal. Less is! It feels great to be freed from the bottomless desire to acquire. I can now appreciate the beauty of everything I see in the stores, but I don't *have to have it.* I can't deny that I still love shopping. But now I pause before the purchase, whereas before I was much more impulsive. Now it's joyful, not compulsive. I don't need it all, and I appreciate so much more the few things that I choose to buy.

What makes me happy? What matters to me? When you meditate, these are the kinds of questions you ask yourself, and the answers lead you to the true meaning and experience of happiness.

Meditation also helps you let go of what you *don't* want or need to make you whole. Bad habits and addictions get left behind. Not through magic; through awareness. Unplug teacher Laurie Cousins specializes in mindfulness-based interventions for addiction. She explains, "When we go into autopilot and do things by rote, we can go to places that are habitual but not necessarily helpful to us. We all have these habitual thought patterns, and that's what leads us to impulsivity. When you build a practice, you are able to observe yourself and ask, *Is this really what I want for myself, long-term?*"

When you're awake, you can pause, slow down, and ask yourself that question before you inhale, swallow, or acquire. You pay attention to what you're doing rather than slipping into mindless acquiring, inhaling, or numbing out with food, drink, gambling, shopping, or anything else. There's good reason meditation is the eleventh step in twelve-step recovery programs.

Speaking of more and more of less and less: Meditation is also great for weight loss (got your attention there, didn't I?). Mindfulness extends to eating, too! A study done by the National Institutes of Health on people who binge eat showed that those who used mindfulness-based tools went from bingeing on average four times a week to only once a week. They also reported feeling more in control when they were around food. You're far less likely to inhale an entire box of doughnuts if you're fully present to what you're doing. As yoga master Steve Ross says — and he's the most disciplined eater I've ever met — when you meditate, the drive to overeat or do things that are self-destructive simply goes away. (Just a quick caveat here as I'm extolling the physical virtues of meditation: It *won't* give you a higher, rounder, or better ass. It may, however, motivate you to get up off yours and do what it takes to get one.)

More and more of less and less . . . trust me, it's so liberating!

Meditation came into my life when I was grieving the recent death of my mom and was just starting my journey as a sober woman. As an active alcoholic for ten years, I was always trying to calm anxieties, find escapes, and quiet my mind. Meditation has taught me about who I am, down to the core. It has helped aid me in my healing of the loss of my mom as well as learn to stay fully present throughout my sobriety. Without meditation, my mind can be a scary space. If I take just a moment to home in and focus on my breath, the chatter stops. Even if it's just a minute, it stops. There is nothing like it. No drug, no drink gave me what meditation has: a calm, an inner peace, and a self-love I didn't have before.

KATIE, 29, COMEDIAN

Your Relationships Will Get Better, Stronger, and Happier

If you look at every problem in the world, it's a result of lack of emotion regulation. When people can't deal with their emotions, they lose their ability to communicate with each other and work together.

NATALIE BELL

Your relationships get better because *you* get better. You get calmer, clearer, more in control of your reactions. You get more patient and more tolerant of others' flaws and quirks as your compassion increases. One of the areas of the brain in which neuroscientist Sara Lazar discovered increased volume as a result of meditation is called the temporoparietal junction, which she explains is connected with empathy, perspective, and compassion.

As all these positive changes happen within you, something amazing happens: *The people in your life reflect these changes back to you.*

This is great news for anyone in a committed relationship, but the benefits go way beyond just your significant other. Your relationships improve with your friends, colleagues, and kids, too. I'm definitely a better mom since becoming a meditator. My boys will attest to that. I used to snap at them, rarely stopping and smelling the children, so to speak, because I was hurrying them along the conveyer belt of daily life. Getting them out the door to the bus every morning was a nightmare for all of us. Now, it's not that I never morph into Momzilla, but I'm aware of it much faster, so I'm able to pause and reset. I stop us at the door and break from mom madness. We take a breath and it changes everyone's day. I can see when I'm reacting to their stress with my own stress, and I step back and do it better. I'm happier, they're happier.

The only downside is that my family is on to me if I skip a day. The truth is that when I don't meditate, I see and feel the results. I'm quicker to lose my patience, and to their credit, my kids call me out on it: "Mom, did you meditate today?" It's annoying, but they can tell when I do and don't. I'd be lying if I said I meditate every single day. But the days when I forget, I regret. And so do the people I love . . . pretty good motivation to stick with it.

You'll Be More Gorgeous

> Meditation gives you the type of glow that makes people stop and say, "I want what she has."
>
> LAUREN ECKSTROM

Meditation is the best-kept beauty secret around.

We all know a smile is the prettiest thing you can wear. When your face is tensed up, you just look . . . well, not gorgeous. But with a regular meditation practice, you'll be naturally happier, and thus naturally gorgeous! Plus, worrying all the time gives you worry lines. Forget Retin-A; the only lotion or potion you need is a few minutes every day in quiet stillness. Take away the worry and you prevent the wrinkles in the first place.

Meditation also makes you sexy. Yes, really. I don't mean cheesy underwear-ad sexy. I'm talking megawatt magnetic. How is this possible, you ask? Because you'll discover the secret to what's truly sexy and what isn't.

Stress just isn't sexy anymore. We all hear people say, "Oh, I'm so crazed," like that's a good thing. But what they don't realize is that it's actually a huge turn-off. To not be able to experience the present moment because you're always running off to the next thing is an energy people don't want to be around.

You know what *is* sexy? Being present.

If you think about anyone you know that just has "it" — you know, that unmistakable something that draws you in and makes them irresistible — you'll realize that "it" is the ability to be fully, genuinely engaged and present. When they're with you, they're *with* you. Their eyes aren't darting around, they aren't checking their cell phone; they're 100 percent focused on you and engaged, even if it's only for that minute. That's *charisma,* and it's the secret sauce to being superstar sexy.

By the way, this has been proven. Harvard psychologist and author Ellen Langer, PhD (nicknamed "the Mother of Mindfulness"), did a study in which two different groups of people sold magazines. One group recited a canned sales script they had memorized, and the other group talked to their potential customers mindfully, personalizing the pitch by changing small details each time. Customers then rated the two groups and said they found those in the mindful group to be much more charismatic and appealing. When you're engaged and present, others experience you as more genuine — and therefore more attractive.

If you ever get the chance to take a class with or meet Steve Ross in person, you'll see what I'm talking about. Steve is the coolest of the cool (and not just because he played guitar for Fleetwood Mac). Everyone wants to be around Steve. He's warm, fun, and funny, and he radiates calm. Nothing rattles him. But more than that, he looks right into your soul when he's talking to you and makes you feel like you're the only person in the universe. You never leave Steve's presence without feeling elevated.

And really, that's what this is all about: how you leave others feeling when they cross your path. The more happiness and peace you feel, the more you'll emit that to others, and the more they'll reflect it back to you.

You'll Make Better and Faster Decisions

When we get to the intuition, we can excavate what it is that we really want. What your soul tells you in meditation: that's intuition.

KRISTEN LUMAN

When I first said I was finished with fashion and opening a meditation studio, people thought I was nuts. They told me that no one would pay to do something they could easily do at home for free. Even some of my family members were question marking my decision. But I just knew in my gut this would work. When you just know something from deep down, you *know*. You don't have to waffle or waver, and suddenly, making decisions is easy.

There are lots of decisions we have to make in life, and being able to *just do it* rather than having the pain of indecision drag on is such a gift. One thing I've learned through this process is that I have to be fair and true to myself. I'm a natural-born people pleaser, which in the past has made me say yes to a lot of things that were beneficial for others but not necessarily so great for me. You want me to drive three hours to speak at a conference where twelve people show up? Sure thing. You want me to do makeovers in the bathroom of Madison Square Garden for the trainers at the Westminster Dog Show (true story)? Absolutely. Never mind that I'm allergic to dogs. Had I been a meditator at that time, I never would have said yes to that!

Meditators trust their gut more because they can actually hear it. We're usually so busy going and doing that we don't slow down enough to tune in to the wisdom we have in there. When we think we don't know the answer to what we should do, or what we want, we actually do — we just can't hear it through all the chatter and static.

Meditation teacher and life coach Heather Hayward put this beautifully:

> Meditation helps make all those voices in our head sit down and allows us to listen to a wiser guidance system. It connects you to that still, small voice within you, and then every decision you make then comes from that connection. Not from a lot of other information and interpretation, but a visceral experience of what you should be doing. If you start to really listen in and feel the signals from your body, you're able to read "I do or don't feel this is right." You don't waste time or energy anymore going down all the different rabbit holes of indecision when you know what voices to listen to.

Now, before I say yes to anything, I tune in to see if it feels right to and for me. When my gut says no, I say no — which is liberating! I know now that my time is valuable and important, so I spend it wisely, and I make decisions according to that. I don't lose my whole day to an overwhelming to-do list anymore. This process allows me to distinguish what I do and don't want to do, instead of reacting and automatically saying yes to everything.

Speaking of what you discover when you tune in and listen . . .

Before meditating, I was quite indecisive and lacking real clarity in most areas of my life, but since I've incorporated meditation that has thankfully changed. It has allowed me to answer questions and make decisions through quieting the mind and relaxing. While my mind is quiet and I focus on the breath, I get a feeling of inexplicable clarity and calmness, which has helped me to create powerful things in my life.

TANAZ, 31, TEACHER AND LIFE COACH

You May Find Your Purpose in Life

When you're stuck in fight/flight mode, your body sends out chemicals that make your peripheral vision narrower. Meditation relaxes you so you can expand your vision — it *literally* broadens your horizons.

LENA GEORGE

Meditation can deliver big moments of clarity. Ideas and thoughts that you didn't even know you had may pop up. Huge realizations and breakthroughs appear. You get those "aha moments" that show up in therapy after talking and talking, except here you didn't have to say a word. We don't usually get to hear those important messages to ourselves because we're so busy doing and thinking rather than just being (yours truly included — I don't *always* slow down enough to hear them — that's why they call this a practice).

When you get still and quiet, you can find out your purpose in life. You see things differently because you unplug from your usual thoughts and plug in to your intuition. I can't tell you how many people have come up to me at the studio to tell me they've made big changes in their life because of realizations they had in meditation. Some have quit their job to pursue what they really love. Some realized it was time to end a difficult relationship that was making them unhappy. Others had huge creative awakenings. One published five books of her architectural photos, which she'd been wanting to do for years. Another wrote a popular television episode based on an idea that came to him while he was meditating.

There's something about meditation that opens up possibilities and paths that you might not have previously imagined but that are utterly right for you.

Meditation teacher Johnny O'Callaghan has an incredible story about how meditation primed him to hear a life-changing message his gut was sending. Johnny was an actor with a thriving career when a friend invited him to go on a trip to Africa. Something in him said that he should go — even though his agent was telling him he would be missing out on a bumper pilot season coming up. Johnny followed his intuition and went. While he was there, he met a young African orphan boy named Odin. When Odin climbed into his lap, Johnny immediately heard in his mind, to his absolute surprise, "This is your son." I probably don't need to tell you that it's now thirteen years later and Johnny has been a happy, utterly devoted father to Odin.

Ram Dass once said, "The quieter you get, the more you can hear." That really sums up what this practice is. It allows us to tune in and listen to ourselves. We get to what we're supposed to be doing once we stop doing whatever we're so busy with and just listen. You don't want to wake up thirty years from now realizing you've spent your whole life climbing up the wrong ladder! Meditating is like waking up your internal personal life coach who directs you to what will truly make you happy and fulfilled.

As Mark Twain said, "The two most important days in a person's life are the day he is born and the day he finds out why."

I'm a former chief operating officer who is currently a stay-at-home mom — a choice I made as a result of meditation. Meditation gave me clarity about my own truth and about what was not working by helping me manage my stress so that I could evaluate my career, future, and desires in an observant rather than reactionary fashion. It also gave me the courage to leave my job without going directly to another, and the confidence to make space for the right next step and to allow myself the time to focus on and claim my motherhood. It also made the "space in between" a comfortable place.

JENNIFER, 47

You'll Feel *Alive*!

Here's how I see this: You can keep going the way you're going, crashing around your to-do list (been there!). Or, you can change the channel and go "live and on the air." That's the part of being on television spots I always loved: You are ON. You're in the moment, and everything you say matters because it is being heard by millions. That's what meditation feels like outside of your sitting sessions. It's just like being on live TV, only you're living your unscripted life in the present moment, in real time. I don't care if you're needlepointing or downhill skiing, you're going to have a far better and fuller experience if you're present while doing it.

Steve Ross says that some people need to risk their lives in order to feel it. But he just meditates and gets to the same place. He doesn't need to jump out of an airplane to feel fully alive. And now, neither will you.

■ ■ ■ ■

UNPLUG AND RECHARGE

■ ■ ■ ■

Don't you already feel so inspired to meditate? I hope so, because you're going to love it!

In this section I'll give you all you need to know about the logistics of meditation: how, when, and where to sit, how to set yourself up for success, what to "do" with the thoughts that come up, and how to troubleshoot some common challenges. I'll also give you lots of tips from experts and meditators on letting go of judgments and expectations. Remember, there's no such thing as a "good meditator," or even a bad meditation. It's all good!

SIT HAPPENS: THE BASICS

So far we've hit the what, why, and who of meditation, as in:

What meditation is (moving from thinking
 to being)
Why it's good for you (you'll get calm,
 focused, healthy, happy, . . . etc.)
Who can do it (anyone, including you)

Just a few more — when, where, and how — and then you're on your way to getting unplugged and recharged . . .

When to Meditate
The best time of day to meditate is first thing in the morning. This isn't just my advice; there's actually some science to this. There are different rhythms of the brain; when we first wake up, we're still in the "theta" brainwave state, in which our brains are most easily reshaped and influenced. We

also enter the theta state right before we fall asleep, so that's another good time to meditate.

But here's another very good reason to meditate first thing in the morning: because then it's DONE! It's the easiest way to make sure you get it in every day. You rise and meditate before you do anything else, and it soon becomes a ritual. Do it before you do anything else, and then there's no chance it'll get eclipsed by the usual chaos of daily life.

After many hours of research and even more hours sitting, I've discovered the insider secret to getting yourself to meditate each morning. Ready? Here it is:

1. Step one: Get up.
2. Step two: Get it done.

That pretty much covers it. If you aren't doing a scheduled guided meditation with a guide, aren't taking a class, and especially if you "don't have the time," this is a surefire way to make it work.

Meditating in the morning sets you up to be calmer, more focused, more productive, and just plain nicer to yourself and others throughout the rest of your day. You'll notice it, and so will everyone around you. By starting your morning with a few minutes of quiet peace, you set yourself up for success because you set an intention to be present. You start your morning with intention and purpose so you can go about your day the way you want it to happen, rather than reacting to every little thing that comes at you.

Having said all that, it doesn't matter when you do it, truthfully, as long as it works for you and your life. Some of our students are stay-at-home moms who like to meditate after the morning rush of getting their kids off to school. We've got screenwriters who work at home and take a midday break to meditate (a lot of them also do quickie sessions if they hit a block). Many people who work in offices have told me they do it as soon as they get home at the end of the day, immediately after changing into comfy at-home clothes. Others drop into the studio at lunchtime to squeeze in a thirty-minute class.

It helps to actually schedule your meditation, just like you would anything else, so it becomes a regular part of your routine. Later on, once it becomes more of an ingrained habit, you can play around with fitting it into your life in more varied ways, but if you're just starting out, pick your regular time and just commit. All in. No skipping it, no deciding if you feel like it that day or not. There will be some days at first when the last thing you feel like doing is just sitting there. But remember, you're not doing it for what happens when you're sitting there. You're doing it for the results it produces in your life when you're not. So just do it. As meditation teacher Heather Hayward says, "You don't take a vote about whether you want to do it or not. You just show up and sit. It's a commitment, not a vote. It's the vote that makes us insane."

The first few weeks may feel a little like a drag. It might be a little uncomfortable, or frustrating, or just plain boring, especially if you feel like it's "not working." Just stick with it anyway (and see page 131 for troubleshooting tips on how to deal with these challenges). Because when you decide to go for it all in, you really will see changes, and then suddenly you'll start craving it. It won't be a struggle anymore to make the time for it, because you'll *want* to do it. And then it becomes as ingrained in your basic routine of self-care as brushing your teeth.

Remember, you don't have to sit for long stretches of time to get the benefits. Just choose the most amount of time you know you'll stick with and not dread or blow off

— even if that's just five minutes at first. Unplug teacher Camilla Sacre-Dallerup says (in her utterly lovely British accent), "Meditation should be a little gift you give yourself — not one you force on yourself." My advice is to start with five to ten minutes a day, then work your way up a few minutes every day until you hit fifteen. (This is what I've found to be my magic number when I meditate alone, or forty-five when I do it in a group. Yours may be a little less or a little more. Feel it out and you'll know.) It really helps to set a timer, even if you're one of those people who have a super-precise internal clock; this way you can fully let go mentally and leave the timekeeping to an electronic device.

I said it before, but I'll say it again, because it's that important: You won't find the time in your busy life to meditate. You have to *make* the time to meditate. It's the only way. Anyone can carve out fifteen minutes to do something if it's important to them — even you. Fifteen minutes: that's half of a mindless sitcom, one chitchat loop around your office, one scroll through Facebook, Instagram, eBay, or whatever your go-to website is. None of those things will make any difference in your life, but fifteen minutes on a cushion daily can change it radically.

Where to Meditate

Anywhere.

I don't believe there is one perfect place to meditate. Anytime you go within, you're going to have a meditation. Some people have a special meditation space, and I'm sure that's an ideal setting, but I've honestly had some of my best meditations in my car in the parking lot of a Bristol Farms supermarket. Beautiful, serene places can be idyllic, but it honestly does not matter where you are once you close your eyes.

Pretty much like everything else about meditation, you need to find the places that work best for you. Your only basic requirements are that it's someplace that's relatively quiet, where you won't be disturbed. It's best to choose a place that you don't associate with high stress. Your office usually isn't the best choice — even if you can lock your door and shut off your phone, it's pretty difficult to turn everything off when you're in the epicenter of your busyness.

You also want to be someplace that's safe. Some people love to meditate in nature, like one of our students who likes to meditate on the beach at sunrise. But for me, although I love the beach, I don't feel quite at peace with my eyes closed and my handbag exposed (remember, I'm a New Yorker). The last thing you want to have to worry about during a meditation is getting mugged. So if you are doing it in a public place, just make sure it's somewhere safe.

> The biggest surprise about meditation practice is the ability to do it anywhere anytime. To just close my eyes, take a breath, and connect is WONDERFUL!
>
> LAUREN, 50, ATTORNEY

How to Sit

There's more advice out there about the mechanics of sitting in meditation than you can even imagine. Sit cross-legged in lotus to hold steady . . . place your hands in your lap in symbolic position to focus the mind . . . sit with a straight spine so the energy of your body flows more freely. It's all kind of fascinating to learn about, but sitting doesn't need to be so complicated to be effective! And it definitely doesn't need to adhere to super-strict guidelines. We need to get over the idea that we need to sit in one prescribed, rigid position, because that's not for everyone.

Here's the essential rundown of how to sit in meditation, to help you find the posture that works best for you:

- **Sit on something comfortable.** Make this easy on yourself! You can use a traditional meditation cushion setup. This is a square flat cushion called a "zabuton," with a round pillow called a "zafu" on top of it. These are great for spine alignment. You can also use a couch, a chair, a floor seat (called a "back jack"), or a folded-up blanket. Some people like to use a meditation bench, but I find these to be less comfortable.
- **Cross your legs . . . or don't.** Some people like to sit cross-legged on a cushion, some like to sit up in bed with their legs out in front of them, some like to sit up straight in a chair with their feet on the floor. Pick whichever feels most natural for you. The only thing you want to make sure is that your legs are at or below the level of your hips (helps to keep them from falling asleep).
- **Rest your hands on your legs . . . or don't.** Some people like to sit with their palms facing up in their lap, because it feels more open and receiving; others like to do palms down to

have more of an internal experience. Some say you should hold your thumb and forefinger in a classic mudra position (such as making a circle with each thumb and forefinger and resting the hands on your thighs, palms facing upward), which can ground your awareness through the sensation of touch. I believe all that to be true. However, I put my hands wherever the heck I want, which is usually crossed in my lap. This is probably not technically correct, but I don't feel any negative impact of that at all. I suggest trying any or all of these, or do whatever you like with your hands as long as they're at rest.

- **Forget sitting altogether and lie down.** Sitting up straight is great because you're in alignment, but I also like lying down in meditation sometimes. I want to be comfortable when I meditate, not worrying if my lower back is bothering me or my foot is falling asleep. The only issue with lying down, obviously, is that you might fall asleep. Although it's great to be relaxed, we want you to be aware and present, not falling asleep. If you're sleeping, you're not meditating. So if you tend to nod off, stick with sitting up. Even sitting up you might doze off, but then your neck will drop forward or backward, which will wake you up. It still happens to me all the time!

Whatever posture you choose, just get comfortable and arrange yourself so you can sit reasonably still. Davidji once told me a story about the time he spent in a Zen monastery, where if you moved at all, you had to raise your hand and the monk would come over and whack it with a stick. He decided to quit Zen when he found himself lying to his Zen master to avoid being hit. We definitely don't do that at Unplug! It's completely fine to shift or adjust if you need to. Just know that the less moving around you do once you close your eyes, the less you distract yourself.

Along those lines, it's helpful to take a minute to do a quick head-to-toe scan before you start, to make sure there's nothing glaring that's going to distract you. Ankle feel tweaky in the position it's in? Fix it now. Nose itch? Scratch it. Pants too tight? Unbutton them. No one's looking.

Lastly, I want to share with you a great insight from teacher Megan Monahan on the whole "sitting still" thing, in case this is something you worry about struggling with:

Really, it's not so much about being able to physically sit still. Although there are some people who have extremely high energy, often what this stems from is that they have a lot of turbulent thoughts, so sitting still physically is not mentally comfortable. But as you keep meditating, you will create more space in between the thoughts, and that turbulence will start to slow down. A lot of the turbulence is you releasing stored stress that has been living in your physical body or your mind. If you're really fidgety in the beginning, that can be your body or mind releasing stored emotional toxicity or stress. It might be uncomfortable in the beginning, but it's not always going to be like that! Just commit to the consistency of it and it'll get easier.

That covers the basics. Next up are tried-and-true tips for setting yourself up for a good sitting session, and then you're ready to start your meditation journey.

MAKE IT EASY

Meditation is easy — and we want to keep it that way! Here are some tips for settling into your sit to make it stress-free.

- **Time It Right.** Pick a time that you likely won't be interrupted. When your Chinese food delivery is imminent, for instance, is probably not the ideal moment. Make sure there isn't anything urgent you need to take care of before you sit (a visit to the bathroom, checking on your kids, getting to the post office before it closes in an hour to mail your quarterly taxes, etc.).
- **Silence Your Phone.** The only vibes you want in your meditation are good ones, so switch off that ringer! As one of our students said after finishing a meditation and checking her phone, "I realized that no one died and the world didn't come to an end while I was

unplugged." I promise, every text, e-mail, or post will be there waiting for you when you're done.

- **Create a Ritual.** Doing the same thing each time before you begin your session signals your brain, *It's time to meditate.* This isn't made-up advice; it's science. A ritual might be sitting in one specific chair or spot in your home, wrapping yourself up in a favorite scarf or blanket, or lighting a candle. My favorite is dropping orange oil in one palm, diffusing it by rubbing my palms together, and then smelling it. Instant shift and I am ready to start! Steve Ross turned me on to this centering ritual, which I also like to use sometimes: Place your thumb on the space between your eyebrows, right above the bridge of your nose. Close your eyes and bring your attention to that spot. That never fails to shut down my brain noise and bring me into the present moment. It just works for me.

- **Do a Brain Drain Before You Begin.** I learned this trick from Julia Cameron's book *The Artist's Way.* Take out a piece of paper and write down all the things you need to do and all the things on your mind. Then put the piece of paper away and sit down to meditate. This way, you won't be worried that you'll forget anything. Plus, when your meditation is finished, you'll be much better equipped to tackle whatever is on that list.

- **Lock It Up.** Similar to the brain drain is our own Camilla Sacre-Dallerup's "locker visualization." Before she became a meditation teacher, Camilla was a lifelong professional ballroom dancer who competed around the world and starred on the British version of *Dancing with the Stars* for six years. Trained by some of the top athletic coaches in the world, Camilla learned this technique so she could leave everything behind and be fully focused and in the moment while performing. Here's what you do: Close your eyes and imagine yourself walking into a locker room. Choose a locker and throw in everything on your to-do list and all your worries — all of it. Take as long as you like. When you're done, imagine yourself closing and locking the door, then walking out of the locker room into a safe, empty space. They are securely left in there for you to pick up at any time after your meditation.

- **Find a Meditation Buddy.** Having someone to be accountable to is a tried-and-true success secret. I did this with a good friend who knew a lot about meditation from me but wasn't actually *doing it.* (Davidji jokes that the smarter someone is, the more they're convinced they get the benefits of meditation just by understanding how it works.) Every day we'd just text a quick "meditation done," and maybe share one or two things that we experienced in our session. It kept us both on track — especially since we had a sworn pact of no lying!

WHAT IF . . . ?

Like anything worthwhile, meditation may come with some challenges. Here are some of the most common issues that come up in meditation practice, and what to do about them. What if . . .

. . . Your Brain Won't Quiet Down.
See "What to 'Do' with the Thoughts" (page 144).

. . . Your Legs Fall Asleep.

You have two choices here. You can move your legs so the tingling isn't distracting you, or ignore them. What you don't want to do is create a whole drama around your legs falling asleep. It's not a big deal, and it's *not* a sign that you're not designed for meditation! If it keeps happening and is bugging you, try these sitting adjustments, which usually help:

1. Sit cross-legged on a bolster cushion, so your hips are raised up slightly higher than your legs.
2. Sit in a chair instead, with your legs bent naturally and your feet on the floor.
3. Or just lie down and forget sitting entirely. I know I keep saying this, but it's really true: It's all about what works for *you.*

. . . You Get Distracted by Noises Around You.

Our studio is on the ground level right on Wilshire Boulevard, a busy main street in Los Angeles. This turned out to be the ideal metaphor for everything that happens in meditation. In the beginning, I was very concerned with what was going on in and around the room. I wanted to create the perfect meditative experience for students (and for myself) that was calm, silent, and serene. No surprise, that didn't happen. Someone would honk their horn outside — I'd get annoyed. I'd get distracted in class by bracelets clanking on the floor, or if someone coughed or moved or snored.

As I started to grow the practice within myself, I stopped caring so much. Not about the quality of students' experiences, but about shielding them from every little distraction. Someone honked? Hmm. Okay. Go back to the breath. Someone coughed? Okay. I'd notice the thought — *poor thing, hope she's not sick* — then go back to the breath. It turned out that the distractions weren't ruining the practice — they were part of it! The thing is, you *want* to let the sounds in, because that's the practice: not hiding from distractions, or thoughts, or feelings, but letting them all in and then letting them pass right on by.

There's no perfect experience of meditation, external or internal. The "perfect experience" is one in which you fully accept things, exactly as they are. You can't control the sounds around you any more than you can stop your thoughts. You can only control your own connection with your breath or mantra, and your reaction to those sounds. Once you realize how your brain works, it becomes an adventure seeing that the outside experience with the world is nothing and the internal experience is everything.

In the beginning, you might have to wait it out a little until the noises or other distractions going on around you don't drive you crazy anymore. Pretty soon you'll be able to notice you're annoyed by a sound, come back to the breath, and let it go. You have to ride the waves of letting the outside distractions go, in the same way you let go of the internal chatter and distractions. We usually start off battling the external distractions (sounds, etc.) and then move to the internal (thoughts or sensations in the body). The journey begins when you're okay just letting both be. The more you do it, the deeper your experience becomes.

. . . You Fall Asleep.
It happens all the time. Nothing to do here, really, other than be grateful that you had a good nap and try again. If you were lying down, I'd recommend sitting up next time, because if you fall asleep in that position, your head will nod forward or back and wake you up.

. . . You're Really, Really Struggling.

And by this, I mean you've applied all the tips and tricks I've given you, and it still feels agonizing. First, bring in one of the foundational attitudes of mindfulness: patience! For more specific tips on having patience with the process and with yourself, see page 151.

It may also be that the style of meditation you've tried might not be the right one for you (no, I didn't say that *meditation* isn't right for you . . . I said that the *style* you tried might not be the right one for you. Remember, there are as many ways to meditate as there are to make an egg!). Meditation teacher Lena George wisely advises, "If any meditation you're doing feels torturous, try another! Otherwise it's counterproductive and you're creating more stress."

If you're using just the breath, try using a mantra. If you're using a mantra, try using an object, like holding a stone, gazing into the flame of a candle, or looking at a flower. Or, you can try guided meditation. See "Other Ways to Meditate" (page 185) for a how-to on all of these styles. There's a meditation path that's right for each person — you may just need to experiment a little to find yours.

THE SIMPLE FORMULA FOR STRAIGHT-UP MEDITATION

Okay, you're sitting and comfortable.

Now what?

The act of meditation comes down to these six steps:

1. Focus on a single point (your breath, a mantra, a sound, or an object).
2. Let your focus go (this happens consciously or unconsciously).
3. Drift in the gap of peace and nothingness that arises (even if it lasts a millisecond).
4. Notice that your thoughts have snuck back in.
5. Bring your attention back to the single point of focus.
6. Repeat.

Literally, that's all there is to it. That's the simple formula that can change your life in a thousand ways for the better. You can take hundreds of classes in all the different disciplines, but you, too, will come to realize that the above formula is all there is.

I'll break down each of the six steps so you can see them in action.

Step One: Focus on a Single Point

If you're using your breath — which is the easiest method because you don't need anything other than something you do every moment of every day — simply notice it flowing in and out of your nose. Not counting or trying to control the breath, just noticing each inhalation and exhalation.

If you'd like to use a mantra, you repeat it to yourself in rhythm with your breath. For those who have a special one, you can use yours, or you can use one of the classic ones below:

Ah hum (*ah* on the in-breath, *hummm* on the out-breath)

So hum (*so* on the in-breath, *hummm* on the out-breath)

I am (*I* on the in-breath, *ammmm* on the out-breath)

Ohm (*ooohhh . . . mmm*)

Ram (*raaa . . . mmm*)

Most mantras are meaningless words, but

the sounds aren't arbitrary. Author and longtime meditator and teacher Mallika Chopra has been a primordial sound practitioner for more than twenty years (and was initially taught to meditate at age nine by her father, Deepak Chopra). She explains that these vibrational sounds have a healing quality, which is why so many traditions use these mantras.

You can also do what meditation teacher Laura Conley calls "BYOM": bring your own mantra. I love creating and collecting personal mantras, because they allow you to program what you want to put into your brain. At this point I have more mantras than I do shoes! To make your own mantra, begin by asking yourself the question, *How do I want to feel right now?* Whatever answer comes up, that's your word or phrase. For instance, it might be *calm.* Then close your eyes and take three slow, extended breaths. On the next in-breath say, "I am," and on the out-breath, say your word. So your mantra would become:

Breathe in: *I am*
Breathe out: *calm*

That's all there is to it. Repeat this mantra until you notice you've drifted off, then return to your mantra and begin again. This is the same Simple Formula for Straight-Up Meditation you learned earlier, only using your personally chosen mantra.

There are other singular focuses you can use, like objects, sounds, or even taste. Using objects in meditation is all about directing your attention through your senses. You want to focus on that object and become fully present with it. Say you're looking at a flower. Really *see* that flower. Try to notice every detail. Or say you're holding a certain stone. Really *feel* and explore the weight and texture of that stone in your hand. Same goes for scent, sound, or even taste. I suggest starting with something you're looking at or holding, and then later on moving into scent and taste. As you become more aware of everything through your practice, you won't believe how incredible a humble little raisin tastes! I'll tell you more about taste, scent, and sound meditations on pages 156, 188, and 192.

Step Two: Let Your Focus Go
This isn't so much something you *do* as it is something that just happens. Even if you tried to maintain your singular focus on your breath, mantra, or object with the laser intensity of a thousand suns, your brain

wouldn't let you. Eventually, your attention will wander and your thoughts will start trickling back in.

But . . . and here comes the most important split second in your whole practice . . .

Step Three: Drift in the Gap That Arises

As you continue to practice, you'll start to notice that a tiny gap opens up in between the moment that you let go of your focus and when the thoughts reappear. Even if it's just for a millisecond, you get to drift in that gap of blissful nothingness. Well, it might feel like nothingness, but it is actually complete awareness of the present moment, exactly as it is. That, my friends, is the pure experience of being fully in the present moment. This is what we call being of "no mind," or "the sweet spot."

You rest in that gap for however long you're given, until . . .

Step Four: Notice That the Thoughts Have Snuck Back In

The instant you realize you're off in thought-land again, you've woken up. Welcome back! Yes, you may have drifted off, but you're suddenly *aware* that you've drifted off, and that's the key. Author Eckhart Tolle says, "The moment you realize you are not present, you are present." Noticing our thoughts allows us to step back and become the observer once again, rather than being carried away by the endless stream of internal chatter.

There's nothing you need to do with the thoughts other than notice them, acknowledge them, and let them be. You aren't looking to push them away; just see them for what they are. This has so much value because you can see what your mind naturally does, where it automatically drifts, how it processes. It's pretty cool, actually, to start to see how your brain works. The magic here is that you are now *aware* of the thoughts, and thus don't get tangled up in your reaction to them.

Then, in order to let the thoughts go and come back to center, you simply . . .

Step Five: Refocus

Come back to your breath, your mantra, or your object, same as you did in Step One. That's it. Just return your attention to the breath, the sound, or the sensation.

However — and this is a big however — do it gently. In other words: no judgment! Letting go of judgment and expectations can be the hardest part of meditation. No berating yourself for drifting off, no feeling defeated that you did it wrong or that you "can't meditate." If you're breathing, focusing, noticing your thoughts, and refocusing, you are meditating.

And now, with your attention focused back on your singular point, you . . .

Step Six: Repeat

Do the whole thing all over again.

Focus, Let Go, Drift, Notice, Refocus, Repeat. That's all you do, again and again and again. That is the uncomplicated act of meditating. I know, you probably wish it were fancier or more exciting, but that's all there is to it.

Here's Davidji's take on the simplicity of the process:

Regardless of whatever else is going on, you keep coming back to the object of your attention over and over. It may sound monotonous or boring, it's not designed to be entertaining. It's designed to be grounding. Meditation is a gentle drifting. As long as you have something to come back to, it doesn't matter how far you drift, because you'll come back. Over time, you start to become more comfortable in the fact that THAT'S IT. That's your practice: drift, come back. Drift, come back.

Really. That's it. You can totally do that, right?

Read on for tips on what to do if your mind won't shut up, and how to have a little patience with the process so you can keep your meditation peaceful and happy. As Mallika Chopra says, "The last thing we want to be stressed out about is our meditation practice!"

What to "Do"
with the Thoughts

Remember, the goal isn't to stop your thoughts. Your only objective is to allow them to come in, notice when they do, and let them fade away so you can go back to your meditation. It's kind of like you're cleaning out. You don't fight the thoughts; you let them in and let them go. You're moving through them rather than suppressing them, to hit that empty state of mind.

It's the "letting go" part that's the challenge, I know. So here are some of the best techniques I've discovered to help you do that.

Redirect, Redirect, Redirect
That's the whole secret to meditation, right there.

I love how Davidji explains this. He says, "When you walk into a dark room, you don't do anything with the dark. You just turn on the light. In meditation, you don't

144

do anything with your thoughts. You just direct your attention to something else."

Lena George has another analogy that always makes me laugh as a parent of three boys. She says, "I think of the mind and attention as a toddler. If you tell him to stop doing something, it won't do much. You have to remove the stimulus and redirect him to something else. Here you're redirecting the toddler in your brain. You're giving him a little toy to lure him in the right direction."

In both cases, the "something else" that you redirect to is your object of attention — your breath, mantra, or object. These are the grounding forces that zip you right back into the here and now. Thought comes up, you notice it and acknowledge it, and then shift your attention. Simple but *very* effective!

So don't worry about what to "do" with the thoughts. What matters aren't the thoughts, necessarily, but whether you're getting trapped in your reaction to them. Each time they pop up, just redirect your attention to your breath, mantra, or object, again and again and again . . .

Visualize to Vaporize

It's helpful to imagine sending thoughts off on their merry way when you realize they've appeared. How? By visualizing. Lots of teachers have different visualization analogies they like to use for this, but some of my favorites include seeing the thoughts as leaves being carried away in the current of a stream, clouds passing by, a ship sailing off into the horizon, a wisp of smoke wafting away.

It's also useful to visualize your breath as a stabilizing force. For instance, your thoughts are the waves, but your breath is the anchor that pulls you back. Here's another example from Heather Hayward that I really like:

Your thoughts are just passengers on the train, but the train itself is your breath. It's okay if the passengers are having a party. Even if you have a drunk guy up at the mic screaming or singing, just ride the train. Eventually, one passenger at a time gets off the train. I call what's in between my ears "Grand Central Station," and in meditation, it morphs into "Serenity Station." There's still movement and stillness at the same time, and it's all perfectly okay.

It's really important to remember that "letting go" isn't the same as pushing the thoughts away. The noticing of what's coming up is every bit as important as letting it go. Those are golden opportunities to become aware of how your brain works and how your thoughts might be sabotaging you. Don't judge those thoughts. Just notice, and then release. That's the "letting be" part of this that is intertwined with "letting go."

So, just to recap:

1. Notice the thought.
2. Let it be.
3. Visualize letting it go (and/or returning to your stabilizing force).
4. Redirect back to your breath, mantra, or object.
5. Repeat as needed.

Shake Your Label Maker

Remember Natalie Bell's tip about labeling a thought or feeling when you notice it? It's an instantaneous way to separate *you* from *your thoughts* and bring you back to being the *observer* of your thoughts. This is pure science: When we label a thought or emotion, the amygdala (the anxiety/worry/fight-or-flight center of your brain) immediately calms down. Then you can switch into the calmer, more rational mind, where all the brilliance and bliss happen.

Here's how this works. There you are, with your monkey mind swinging from branch to branch, when POP! You realize you're off on a tangent or in an emotional whirl. Then you give it a name:

"I'm worrying."
"I'm feeling guilty."
"I'm fantasizing."
"I'm getting tense."

One of our students uses what she calls the "Oh, there I go again" technique. As soon as she catches herself in a thought stream, she gives it a label like:

"Oh, there I go again making lists."
"Oh, there I go again worrying about work."
"Oh, there I go again mentally redecorating my house."
"Oh, there I go again feeling envious."
"Oh, there I go again rehearsing what I'm going to say."

What I love about this is that it lets you gently (aka without judgment) let yourself off the hook with a bit of humor. It's okay to laugh at yourself a little. Meditation doesn't have to be so serious! This technique also gives you a lot of insight into how your brain works, so you can become aware of your mental defaults and habits.

Be Nice to Your Brain

You may be a type A person who is used to making things happen, but you can't make anything happen in meditation. You can't *force* your brain to be quiet. So give yourself a break and stop berating that monkey mind for swinging into action.

If your brain just won't shut up, thank it. I'm not kidding. It's doing you a big favor if it's going a million miles a minute while you're meditating. It's showing you in real time how much the chatter in your brain is running the show. It's also giving you the golden opportunity to redirect your attention with purpose, away from the thought stream and back to your breath. And as you now know, this is the simple action that in time rewires your brain.

Besides, as Steve Ross says, "[t]he agitation of your mind is your best friend. Without it, you wouldn't be searching or seeking; you'd just be lying somewhere by the pool. On a soul level, agitation is a sign from your intuition that there's something more to be discovered."

Meditation is the simplest thing in the world, but also the most difficult because the mind will give you a million reasons not to do it. And because our minds are saying not to do it, we tend to think that we are telling this to ourselves. But *sit regularly,* even in short bursts, and you soon start to observe that your mind isn't you, and that a lot of what it says isn't in your best interest.

ART, 41, TELEVISION EXECUTIVE

On Having Patience with the Process (and with Yourself)

Worried that it's "not working"? This is pretty common. I promise you it is, more than you know. But it can still feel frustrating if you feel like you're not getting anywhere. It's not easy for high-achievers to accept that you can't "win" at meditation. You can't even be good at it, really. And trust me, I'm a very competitive person!

Sometimes in meditation you connect to your inner soul and find bliss; sometimes you just sit quietly, breathe, and get calm; and sometimes you sit and feel like it's you versus your racing mind. Any of these experiences can show up on any given day, and the beauty is that it really doesn't matter. One of our regular students, an attorney named Lauren, asked me to share this: "The best advice I have for beginners is that it all counts. Even if your head is going the entire time, it counts. I'm so glad I was told that, so I'm passing it on."

The bottom line is that you'll get all the brain-changing benefits of meditation regardless of whether you see it as a "good" sit or not. I was recently watching an interview on *Good Morning America* with Transcendental Meditation teacher Bob Roth. He recounted a story about his teacher, the Maharishi Mahesh Yogi. A reporter asked the Maharishi, "Some meditations are more on the surface and some meditations seem deeper. Are the deeper ones better?"

"No," the Maharishi answered. "They are both equally good."

When the reporter asked how that was possible, the Maharishi replied, "Because even in a shallow dive, we get wet."

Here are some words of wisdom from our teachers on letting go of judgment and having a little patience with the process . . .

For many people, the first time they sit down, they're making lists. The second time, they're thinking about how they're doing it wrong. The third time, they're thinking about a conversation they had. That's it . . . forget it! They're out. Most of us are driven by effort and focus; we believe that's the magic formula of how we achieve and accomplish. So we approach meditation with that same skill set and feel frustrated that it's not working. But this is the opposite. This is surrender. Can you let go of all the effort and focus and just be with yourself?

— Davidji

It doesn't matter what happens in your meditation. It's kind of like Vegas . . . what happens in your meditation stays there. The benefit of your practice shows up in the rest of your day anyway, so no judgments of how this experience should feel for you.

— Megan Monahan

If I had a weather report of meditation, it would definitely not be like Palm Springs, where it's sunny all the time, or like Seattle, where it's always raining. It would be like Hawaii — bright sun one minute, then rainstorms, and then back again, and it's all perfectly okay. The judgment of whatever happens is what chokes happiness — just the simple happiness of *Hey, I did my five minutes today.*

— Heather Hayward

When you sit down to meditate, your intention only needs to be to experience that meditation, as it happens, without commentary. You're in no position to judge your meditation. What do you know, really, of what's happening and how far along you are in the process?

— Steve Ross

15 DAILY MEDITATIONS

Once you experience what meditation can do for you, you will want that feeling more and more. These mini meditations are the ideal way to get in little hits of focus, calm, and joy throughout your day. You can pick and choose the ones you need whenever you need them. We made all of these short, sweet, and doable in under five minutes, to make it easy for you to work them into your day, but you can always extend these to twenty minutes or more if you have more time. There's nothing stopping you from making any of these into fuller, longer sits for an even deeper and better experience. You can find recordings of each of these meditations on unplugmeditation.com.

The Unplug Meditation

Time it takes: Less than 1 minute
Ideal for: A quick reconnect with yourself

Use this when: You want a little hit of that meditation magic

Each of the other mini meditations you'll find below is for a specific purpose, but this is our quickie classic that sums up all of the other meditations in one. Think of this as your basic go-to whenever you have sixty seconds or less and want to do a centering check-in with yourself. Bonus: It's super-easy to remember!

Here are your steps, which spell out the word *UNPLUG:*

1. U = Unplug your devices and from any tasks you're doing.
2. N = Notice how you're feeling.
3. P = Pick a point of focus (your breath, or a mantra, object, or visualization).
4. L = Let it go.
5. U = Understand that thoughts will come and go.
6. G = Get on with your day!

The Savoring Meditation

Time it takes: 1 minute
Ideal for: Slowing down, appreciating the moment, and experiencing food joy

Try this when: You're beginning a meal or snack

Eating is something we do every single day, usually mindlessly. Be honest: How many times have you sat in front of the television and gone through an entire bag of potato chips, or eaten a cookie and wondered, *Where did it go?* Not only does this take us out of the present moment — it also packs on the pounds because we're not paying attention to what we're shoveling in our mouths.

Eating and meditating at the same time allows you to notice when your body says, *Okay, that's enough now.* I tend to chow down quickly and eat three times as much as I need because I don't give myself the opportunity to notice I'm full. So by the time I get done, I feel sick. This savoring meditating forces you to slow down, which tunes you back in to how much and what you're eating. Even better, you get to actually enjoy your food.

You can do this quick meditation anywhere, anytime, with any food. I'll show it to you here with a raisin, which is how I learned it, so you get the idea. If you even do this for one meal or one snack a day, it's a chance to steal a moment back and do

157

something good for yourself.

Here's the how-to for the savoring meditation, step-by-step:

1. Grab a raisin.
2. Look at the raisin and ask yourself,
   *How did this get from the earth to my
   fingers?* Think about it. Someone
   planted the vines, picked the grapes,
   dried them into raisins . . . imagine
   all the steps it took for this little
   raisin to travel all the way to you.
3. Lift that little raisin to your ear. I
   know it sounds weird, but when you
   squeeze a raisin, it makes a *snap,
   crackle, pop* sound. Spend a few
   seconds listening.
4. Put the raisin in front of your mouth
   with your lips closed. Notice you're
   salivating a little in anticipation. It's
   so weird how that happens, but it
   really does!
5. Place it in your mouth and feel the
   texture with your tongue, then begin to chew as slowly as you possibly can. Notice as you chew how
   the skin separates from the sweet
   inside. I'm sure you never chewed
   anything slowly enough to notice
   how your tongue moves all over on

its own. There's a party going on in your mouth with every bite that you've been invited to all along . . . you just never bothered to RSVP!
6. Swallow, smile, and go on with your day.

Walking Meditation

Time it takes: 3 minutes
Ideal for: Getting grounded; also great for anyone who has trouble sitting still
Try this when: Life feels chaotic, over-whelming, or out of control

We all have those moments: Nothing is going right at work, your kids are driving you crazy, and you just lost your keys for the sixth time this week. To get regrounded amid the chaos, try this walking meditation:

1. Stand up. You can do this meditation in flat shoes, socks, or, ideally, barefoot.
2. Feel your feet. Wiggle your toes and connect to the sensation of the soles of your feet on the ground.
3. Very slowly, lift your right foot and take a step with your right foot. Land with your heel first, then

slowly roll onto the ball of your foot.

4. Take your next step with your left foot the same way, in slow motion. Notice how your weight shifts forward and your body and knees work in tandem like a machine, propelling you forward.

Keep your eyes open and softly focused on a point slightly in front of you; closing them will make you nauseated and dizzy.

Some people do walking meditations for a whole hike, but I don't have the patience for that. Three minutes does the trick for me. I really should have called this book "The Impatient Person's Guide to Meditating"!

A Quick Shot of Calm

Time it takes: 1 to 5 minutes
Ideal for: Relieving anxiety, cooling off anger, or releasing frustration
Try this when: Tensions are running high

For immediate calm when you need it most, try this Espresso Meditation created by our own Johnny O'Callaghan. It is a breathing meditation that hits you just as fast and potently as any jolt of espresso, only this *de-*jitters you. As Johnny explains, "This unplugs you from your mind and into presence. It's great if you're about to give a speech, have to make a tough, fast decision, or go onstage — anytime you need to get present and calm, fast."

Here's how it works:

1. Take seven slow breaths, inhaling through your nose and exhaling through your nose.
2. Take seven more slow breaths, inhaling through your nose and exhaling through your mouth.
3. Finally, take seven more slow breaths, inhaling through your mouth and exhaling through your mouth.

So it goes: in nose/out nose for seven breaths; in nose/ out mouth for seven breaths; in mouth/out mouth for seven breaths. When you're finished, resume breathing normally and notice how your energy has shifted.

Mood Lifter Meditation

Time it takes: 1 minute
Ideal for: Shifting out of a bad mood

Try this when: You're feeling sad, toxic, or annoyed

Gratitude is the instant antidote for a bad mood. You literally cannot feel grumpy and grateful at the same time. Here's how to go from feeling icky to inspired in under sixty seconds:

1. Close your eyes.
2. Think of three people or things you are grateful for. Don't phone this in! You want to choose three things you *genuinely* feel grateful for. It might be someone special in your life, someone who gave up their seat for you on a crowded subway, your kids' health, that it's not raining today . . . it doesn't matter whether it's big or small — it all counts. Coffee is sometimes on my list, for instance.
3. Open your eyes.

Done! It's that easy.

Feel the Love Meditation

Time it takes: 3 to 5 minutes
Ideal for: Increasing or restoring good feelings toward yourself and others

Use this when: You're feeling down on yourself or angry/upset with someone else

This is a classic meditation, often called a "loving-kindness meditation." Whatever you call it, the basic principle is feeling love for yourself and others. It's helpful to use when you're at odds with someone in your life, because it helps you find your way to compassion and back to love. And, really, there's no better feeling than love.

Here's the step-by-step of how to do it:

1. Close your eyes.
2. Turn your attention to yourself and list three things you love about yourself. Are you kind? Are you smart? Are you creative? Do you make people laugh?
3. Next, think of someone who is very dear to you. You probably have many people you love, but for the sake of this meditation, pick the one who is in this minute front and center for you. Imagine yourself hugging them and sending them love.
4. Next, think about a friend who needs a little love. Maybe they're

163

struggling or going through something tough right now. Imagine sending him or her love in the form of a letter; picture them opening it, reading, and then smiling.

5. Now think about someone you feel neutral about. For me, I always think about the receptionist at my kids' school. She's lovely, but not someone I know well. Send this person a little love, visualizing sending them a meaningful appreciation card as a surprise to make them happy.

6. Lastly, think about the person you find the most challenging right now. It's hard to send someone you don't like love, but by doing it, you're actually letting go of your own toxic anger and moving forward. Imagine what it is like to be them, even if that's not something you would want to be. Send them *peace, love, it's all good* thoughts.

This last step cuts away your difficult emotions so you can move forward. Forgiveness or letting go of negative feelings toward someone (or toward yourself) is usually a hard thing to do, but if you follow these steps, it's much easier because you've already cultivated that feeling of love in your heart in steps 1 to 5.

For other variations on a loving-kindness meditation, you can find two of my favorites from Sharon Salzberg or Tara Brach on YouTube.

The Starbucks Meditation

Time it takes: However long the coffee line is
Ideal for: Squeezing in a meditation
Use this when: You're waiting in line . . . and wating . . .

Why waste time in line when you can turn it into an opportunity? We don't even realize how many precious moments we can steal back. Usually, when we're waiting in line, our brain is off on another planet. But with this meditation, you're going to bring it back to this one so you can anchor yourself and recapture the power of being present. Being mindful when you're doing anything is a way of sneaking in meditation in life's everyday moments. We want you to be mindful of the moment you're in, because then you're actually living in the now.

The Starbucks Meditation is a combination of three meditations in one: the Walking Meditation, the Feel the Love Meditation, and the Savoring Meditation. Here's how to make your next caffeine run into a mini mindfulness retreat:

1. As you're standing in line waiting to order, focus on your feet. Literally put all your attention on your feet and feel how they connect to the ground.
2. Very slowly, lift your right foot and take a step with your right foot. Land with your heel first, then slowly roll onto the ball of your foot.
3. Take your next step with your left foot the same way, in slow motion. Notice how your weight shifts forward and your body and knees work in tandem like a machine, propelling you forward. Do this all very slowly — which will be pretty easy since there's someone in front of you in line.
4. When it's your turn to order, look kindly into the eyes of your barista and, with a smile, place your order. If you smile at them, they're going to smile back — that's a connection. It's funny how often we don't

do that. Sometimes they'll even throw in the cappuccino for free. *#ithappens*

5. After your transaction, continue your mindful walk over to the waiting area. Instead of being annoyed with how long it's taking to get your coffee, just stand and connect with your breath. No cheating and reaching for your phone! The battle there is that you want to do anything other than really be there, but you're using that redirect muscle you've been building in your practice to keep bringing yourself back to the present moment.

6. When your drink arrives, pause after you pick it up and feel the heat or cold of it in your hands. Place it under your nose and breathe in the scent. Then sip it, really savoring the taste.

That's how easy it is to turn a forced slow moment into a mindfulness opportunity. I love this quickie meditation — it's such a powerful way to start your day.

Relaxation Meditation

Time it takes: 5 minutes
Ideal for: Releasing tension
Use this when: You need a breather to relax, revive, and refresh

We don't realize half the time that our shoulders are up at our ears and our forehead is all wrinkled. We're tense, and we don't even know it. This body scan meditation is a fantastic way to release the tension throughout your body. We release the tension, and we feel better. It's that simple.
Here's how:

1. Lie down and close your eyes. If you're in your office or anywhere it's not appropriate to lie down, sit up comfortably in a chair.
2. Take three slow, extended breaths.
3. Bring your attention to your feet and notice how they feel. Feel the weight of the back of your heels on the ground. Tense up your feet, then consciously relax them.
4. Slowly work your way up your body in the same way, to your calves, thighs, hips, hands, stomach, chest, arms, shoulders, neck, and face.

Tense your whole leg, then relax it;
you can do this one or both legs at
a time, depending on your time
constraints. Tense your stomach,
then relax those muscles. Make
your hands into fists and relax
them. Go from the bottom up, ending with your face. Relax your lips,
your cheeks, your eyes, your forehead, and your brain.
5. Take one last deep breath and then
open your eyes.

Note: This meditation is also great to do
before sleep, to help you relax and get
yourself to bed.

Meditation for Sound Sleep

Time it takes: 3 minutes
Ideal for: Unwinding before bed
Use this when: You need help getting to
sleep or just want even better sleep

Try this breathing exercise I learned from
Unplug teacher Sara Ivanhoe, then follow it
up with the body scan, and you may be fast
asleep in minutes.

1. Lie down and close your eyes.

2. Take the first and second fingers of your right hand and place them on what's called your "third eye," the spot between your eyebrows and up about 1/2 inch. If you're hitting the middle of your forehead, that's too high. This is a good meditation to check out on our website, unplug-meditation.com, so you can see it in person.
3. Place your right thumb over your right nostril.
4. Slowly breathe into your left nostril, for as long as you can.
5. Then release your thumb and hold your left nostril down with your right pinky, breathing out your right nostril.
6. Alternate in this way, breathing in one nostril and out the other for three minutes, and you'll feel transformed!

The Obsession Obliterator Meditation

Time it takes: 1 to 3 minutes
Ideal for: Breaking free from mental spirals
Use this when: Something is bugging you and you just CAN'T LET IT GO

We all have stuff we obsess over. Mistakes

we've made, feeling fat, worrying about something at work . . . it can be hard to let these things go, but you're now trained to do exactly that! You've worked that muscle of redirect, and this mini guided imagery meditation will help move that along even faster.

Here's what to do next time you can't seem to stop ruminating on something:

1. Close your eyes and think about what you're obsessing over (not hard, right?).
2. Picture a computer screen, with your hand on a mouse or track pad. Direct the arrow to that topic in your imagination and click on it.
3. Imagine dragging that item to your Trash folder. Literally see it get sucked into the digital trash bin.
4. Now hit Empty Trash.
5. Imagine a blank, clean, clear page appearing on the screen, and breathe.
6. If a pop-up of the topic reappears, simply view, drag to Trash, and repeat.

Back-in-Focus Meditation

Time it takes: Less than 1 minute
Ideal for: Regaining focus
Use it when: You realize you've taken a brain hike and need to get back on track

I can't tell you how many meetings I've sat through in which my brain has taken a hike, only to come back not having any idea of what we discussed. Admittedly, this happens to me in conversations, too. When you notice your brain has gone on its own little excursion, here's how you bring it back. This is what's called the STOP meditation, which I learned at the UCLA Mindful Awareness Research Center:

1. **S**top what you're doing.
2. **T**ake a breath — or two, or three, or four.
3. **O**bserve the situation. Notice what's happening, where you are, who is speaking, that you've wandered.
4. **P**roceed with what you're doing — only now do it awake and aware.

Use STOP as often as you need to get yourself back to the here and now.

172

Weight Loss Meditation

Time it takes: 1 to 5 minutes
Idea for: Curbing cravings
Use this when: The doughnuts/French
fries/ice cream are screaming, *Eat me!*

When we overeat or eat things that are bad for us, it is usually because we are stressed and mindlessly caving in to our cravings. We may feel powerless against the temptation of sugar or salty snacks, but we *do* have a choice about what we put in our mouths — and we *can* respond to that strong desire to overeat in a better way, with a little help from our unplugged brains.

If you really want to lose weight, the greatest thing you can do is meditate before meals. Literally put it on your schedule for 7 am, 12 noon, and 6 pm. Starting the day with meditation activates your inner Pause button so you take back control in the moment when temptation hits. You are training your brain to give you a moment to choose consciously before you mindlessly inhale that food.

Here's your in-the-moment meditation when you're in that paused moment, to allow you to make the best choice:

1. Close your eyes and take three long, slow, deep breaths.
2. Repeat these five sentences to yourself (if you have to read them until you commit them to memory, it's fine to open your eyes):

> I eat consciously and am aware of my eating habits.
> I know what makes me feel good and what does not.
> I choose what to put into my body and what not to.
> I eat to nourish myself and to feel good.
> I have the power to say yes and no.

3. Then silently repeat the mantra *I choose.*
4. Repeat this as many times as you need to until the craving quiets down and you feel back in control. Those doughnuts have nothing on you now!

Clarity Meditation

Time it takes: 1 minute
Ideal for: Accessing answers and inspiration from within
Use this when: You're stuck on a problem or question

You're stuck . . . not sure what to do or how to proceed . . . your mind is drawing a blank. Whether it's a personal problem or a creative block you're trying to figure out, this intention meditation is the ideal way to bust through confusion into clarity.

With this meditation, you're using one part of your mind to pose the question or problem, and then shifting into your deeper meditative mind to access the solution. The answer is hidden in there — and meditation can help you find it!

The next time you feel stuck, try this:

1. Close your eyes and take three extended breaths.
2. Think of the question you're pondering.
3. Ask yourself, *What is the answer to this question?*
4. Let go of the question, and begin your regular meditation and notice what comes up for you. If the question continues to pop up, treat it like any other thought and gently let it go, then return to your breath/mantra.

The point isn't to mull over the question — you've probably done enough of that already. You want to let go of the consciousness that created the problem or question so you can drift into the space of awareness where the answers lie.

Tip: Use a few drops of peppermint essential oil, which promotes mental clarity (see Aromatherapy Meditation, page 188).

Chakra Balancing Meditation

Time it takes: 5 minutes and up
Ideal for: Overall balancing of mind, body, and spirit
Use this when: You're feeling "off" or just want a tune-up

Chakras are energy points in your body. You can feel them, but you can't see them. As Steve Ross explains, "Everyone is familiar with the physical body, but there are subtler dimensions. The subtle body — which is the body you're in when you're dreaming — contains seven chakras, or energy vortexes. If you dissect the body, you won't find chakras; but if you dissect the brain, you won't find emotions or thoughts, either. Just because you can't see them doesn't mean they aren't real."

The seven chakras go in a line up your body, beginning at the base of your spine and ending at the crown of your head. Each chakra has a corresponding energy and color. For easy reference, take a look at the following chart:

CHAKRA	LOCATION	ENERGY	COLOR
1st (root)	Base of the spine	Grounding, survival, protection	Red
2nd (sacral)	Between the navel and the pubic bone	Sensuality, creative energy, courage	Orange
3rd (solar plexus)	The midsection	Personal power, abundance	Yellow
4th (heart)	Center of the chest	Love, trust	Green
5th (throat)	Throat area	Communication, self-expression	Blue
6th (third eye)	Between the eyebrows	Intuition, ideas, thoughts, dreams	Indigo
7th (crown)	Crown of the head, or slightly above it	Enlightenment, higher consciousness	Violet

This meditation brings all the different energies into alignment. Everyone loves this one — it's amazing for overall balance. Really, what could be bad about feeling more grounded, more blissful, more empowered, more love, more tuned in, or more enlightened?

Here's Steve's how-to:

1. Lie down and close your eyes.
2. Begin by taking three slow, extended breaths to settle into your body.
3. You're going to scan your chakras twice — the first time you're basically self-diagnosing your body and energetic situation, and the second time you're bringing everything into balance. To do the diagnostic scan, focus and hold your attention on your first chakra, at the base of your spine, to the exclusion of everything else. Notice if you feel a heat, or coolness, a pulsation, or any other sensation associated with holding energy there. If you do, great; that means that chakra is active. If you don't, that's fine, too; it just means you'll want to focus on that one more the second time around to help light it up. Don't get caught up in a whole story about its being active or not. Just notice, let it go, and move on to the next chakra. Work your way up the remaining chakras in the same way, noticing which ones you feel and which ones you don't.
4. Let it all go and take a few more breaths.

5. Bring your focus back to your first chakra to begin your second scan. This time, keep your focus on that chakra for a few minutes. It helps to visualize the color for each one as you're doing this. If your attention wanders, just bring it back to that location and start again. Notice any sensations that come up when you do this, then let them go and refocus on that spot. Work your way up through the remaining six chakras in the same way.

You want to have all the chakras lit up, and in order for that to happen, you need to focus your attention on each one. You'll notice some days you will feel certain chakras very tangibly, and others you don't; each one is a clue. Sometimes, my throat chakra is the only one I'm feeling. I tune in and find that there's something I need to communicate — some truth I need to own up to and speak.

And then the next day, it may be completely different. As you continue to practice this, you'll notice that it changes — what was active one day may be dormant the next. This meditation allows you to balance whatever needs more energy in that particular moment in time.

Tip: You can also lay crystals on one or more chakras for an extra energy boost. It's one of my absolute favorite things to do. See page 199 for more on this.

The Traffic Meditation

Time it takes: 1 to 3 minutes (can be repeated as many times as needed)
Ideal for: Dissolving frustration, stress, and road rage
Use this when: You're in traffic hell

There is nothing more stressful than being stuck on I-405 at 5 p.m. in Los Angeles! Here's our remedy for those times when you see an endless stream of stopped cars ahead of you and start to feel your blood boil. It's literally as easy as A, B, C:

1. A = Attention to the road. Focus on the situation and register complete awareness of the situation, with as much detail as you can. For example: *I am in bumper-to-bumper traffic; I am not moving; I am stuck; I am going to be late and I hate being late; I am miserable.*
2. B = Body scan. Starting with your

feet, scan your entire body to ground yourself. Feel your feet on the pedals, your rear in the seat, your hands on the wheel, and your eyes' gaze on the road.

3. C = Connect with your breath. First, breathe in and out deeply and slowly, in through your nose and out through your mouth. Then, place your attention on your rib cage and inhale to a count of four, feeling it swell. Hold for a count of four, then exhale to a count of four, feeling your rib cage deflate. Count to four and repeat the process a few more times, until you feel yourself relax.

After your ABCs, repeat the mantra *It is what it is* three times, either silently or out loud. The traffic may not disappear but your agitation will.

■ ■ ■ ■

KEEP IT GOING

■ ■ ■ ■

Once your soul gets awakened through meditation, you tend to want to keep going deeper and doing more. There are so many interesting paths to explore out there!

Here you'll find information on other forms of meditation, including guided awareness meditation, aromatherapy meditation, crystal meditation, sound meditation, and intention meditation. I have also included information on five other practices I think are really worth trying: tapping, crystal healing, breath work, sound baths, and meditation for kids. I say try them all to see what you love. You have nothing to lose but your skepticism and stress.

Other Ways to Meditate

I honestly believe that the Simple Formula for Straight-Up Meditation is the easiest way to get your meditation practice going. And, at the same time, meditation is not a one-type-suits-all kind of thing. It's good to try out different ways of meditating to see which you like best. Plus, it makes it fun!

Here are some of my other favorite ways to meditate; you'll find how-to videos for many of these on our website, unplugmedi tation.com.

Guided Awareness Meditation

I love guided imagery. Some people question whether it's actually "meditation," but to me, it absolutely is. Guided imagery is very effective for relaxation and getting calm, and for cultivating positive emotions like gratitude and compassion, but it can also open you up to awareness of situations or inner truths you didn't even know were in there. It is truly a journey to self-discovery. In some guided imagery classes, I have imagined my future self, felt the sensation of lying on a beach in Jamaica, and seen my ideal life up on a movie screen. I've envisioned the tree of my life and myself as the gardener, picking off leaves that represent people I need to let go of or things that I no longer need. I've visualized my dreams accomplished — in detail, discovered desires I never knew I had, and caught glimpses of the depths of my soul in these beautiful forty-five-minute sessions. It is *very* cool!

In guided awareness meditation, you're using the same basic formula you just learned (focus, let go, drift, notice your thoughts have wandered, refocus, repeat) — only instead of using your breath or mantra, you're using the voice of a teacher, who guides you on a visualization journey. You can't get there alone on this one; you do need a good guide. It can be a live teacher, or a recording. I've listed a few favorite sources on our website, unplugmeditation-.com; there are a lot of great ones out there to choose from.

Kristen Luman is a certified hypnotherapist and a guided imagery expert. I love how she explains the promise of guided imagery:

Guided imagery is really a self-discovery process. People experience and see things they may not have expected, and therefore they learn more about themselves. I'll have them imagine, for instance, painting a landscape of their life as it is right now. They might have gone in feeling sunny, but suddenly they see they're painting storm clouds. Okay, so now that you've seen it, how are you going to paint a brighter sky and rolling hills instead of jagged rocks? Whatever you see that you don't want to see, you can change. It's a process of connecting to yourself on that deeper level and creating new, positive associations.

The same areas of the brain light up when we actually do something as light up when we imagine doing that same thing. In this way, you are programming your brain, even in a small way. Our thoughts affect everything, so why not create the thoughts to create the world you want to live in? Why not be the artist of your own masterpiece?

Many beginners find guided meditation to be an easy entry point, since you have someone literally talking you through the journey. Having a guide not only keeps you grounded in something outside of your wandering thoughts but it also gives you the unique connected feeling we get at Unplug that comes from meditating with others.

Aromatherapy Meditation

Scent is a very powerful trigger for the brain. Think about when you walk into a spa. That soothing, refreshing scent signals, *Relaxation is on the way,* and you immediately start to feel more relaxed. I love incorporating essential oils into my meditation practice.

In aromatherapy meditation, you are using scent as your gateway away from your chattering mind and back into the present moment. Here's how it works:

Choose a good-quality essential oil that you like, which you can find at pretty much any natural food or beauty store or online. Here are some favorite essential oils and what each one is particularly good for:

- **Lavender:** relaxation
- **Orange:** happiness, relief from anxiety (my personal favorite)
- **Peppermint:** mental clarity, alertness, and stress relief (also great for headaches)

- **Rose:** heart opening, love, compassion
- **Vanilla:** warmth, comfort

Place a few drops of the oil in the palm of one hand and very slowly rub both hands together to diffuse and release the scent. Bring your hands to your nose, inhale, close your eyes, and focus on the aroma. Then drop your hands, let go, breathe, and follow your meditation practice. As soon as you notice your thoughts have crept back in, lift your hands back toward your face, inhale your scent, and begin again.

What's especially cool is that you can keep the essential oil on your hands and breathe it in whenever you need some recentering throughout the rest of your day. Over time, especially if you use the same scent often, it'll turn into an automatic trigger and immediately put you into the calm (or happy, or invigorated, or loving) state of mind. I really do hope you try using aromatherapy in your meditation. It adds something very special to the experience.

Crystal Meditation

So many people get turned off by the word *crystal.* But crystals are just stones. They aren't magic (unless *magic* means something's effects can be felt but not proved, in which case they are). What I can tell you as a point of proven fact is that they emit measurable frequencies that can be powerful; that's why they are used in lasers and in quartz watches. There are some people who swear they have been healed by crystals (for more on crystal healing, see page 199). Others — like me, for instance — can physically feel a tingling sensation going up their arm when they hold certain ones. I have amethysts in all my kids' rooms, and I do believe it calms them down. As you can see, I'm a believer!

In meditation, crystals can be used as a focal point, the same as you would use your breath or a mantra. When you drift off into thinking about the past or the future, feeling the weight, texture, and sensation of a crystal in your hand is an immediate reminder to let go of those thoughts and return to your breath.

Begin by choosing a crystal. Crystal meditation teacher Jona Genova says buying them in person is best, because you want to pick up the stone and feel it. You can find crystals in specialty stores, many yoga studios, or even some nature centers and gardening shops. If you need to buy one online for convenience, just be sure it's from a boutique that specializes in crystals and minerals, rather than buying from a generic retailer, to ensure you're getting authentic pieces of the highest quality.

Each type of crystal embodies a specific energy. Rose quartz, for example, facilitates giving and receiving love; amethyst promotes feelings of calm. However, Jona feels strongly that when you choose your crystal, you should do it intuitively, without reading first the description of its properties or powers. Almost always you'll find that the stone you chose represents the energy and qualities you want to bring into your life.

The top six most popular stones at Unplug are these:

1. Rose quartz: love
2. Amethyst: calming
3. Black tourmaline: grounding
4. Clear quartz: all-around balancing that amplifies energy (like the energy of joy, the energy of calmness, and so on)
5. Carnelian: happiness
6. Pyrite: success, good luck, and prosperity

Once you've chosen your crystal, get comfortable in your favorite meditation position and hold your stone in your hand.

Another option is to lie down and place it on a part of your body (see page 202 for more about matching crystals to different chakras and locations on your body). Close your eyes, take a breath, and focus on your stone. Really feel its weight, temperature, and texture. Focus on your stone and breathe, let go, and drift. When you notice your thoughts have crept back in, bring your awareness back to the sensation of the crystal and begin again.

Oh, and if you think meditating with a crystal is powerful, wait until you try a full-body crystal healing! It uses the power of these stones to balance and heal you on every level. You can read more about this on page 199.

Sound Meditation

If you've never meditated to the sound of a Tibetan singing bowl, I highly recommend trying it. For me, sound meditation is one of the most exciting ways to meditate, because you can physically feel it. Instead of focusing exclusively on your breath, you're focusing on the sensation of sound vibration, which helps you tune out your brain and tune in to yourself.

There are a few ways you can do this. First, you need to get yourself a bowl, which you can easily find online. It doesn't need to be anything fancy, or much bigger than a soup bowl. Most come with a small wooden mallet, which you'll also need.

Next, lie down and place the bowl on your chest or stomach. Take a few slow, extended breaths to settle in, and then hit the edge of the bowl with the mallet. You'll immediately hear a beautiful, melodious sound, but even more, you'll feel the vibration go through your whole body. Trust me, it's amazing! Direct your attention to the sound and the sensation and use those as your focal point for your meditation. When it stops, sit in silence and awareness. When your mind wanders, simply hit the bowl and begin again.

Experiment by placing the bowl on different parts of your body, because each one produces its own sensation. Gonging the bowl on your bare feet, for instance, feels like you're dunking them in a bath of warm water. You can also do what's called a "sound shower." This is not to be done in public, because people will think you're crazy, but it's definitely to be done! Place the bowl upside down on your head and then hit it gently. The sound will shower down all over your body. A sound shower is one of the easiest and fastest ways to totally chill yourself out.

On page 206 I'll tell you about sound baths, which take sound meditation to a whole other level. A professional plays a series of gongs and bells that embody the sound of the universe, and you float off into the dreamiest meditative state you can possibly imagine.

Intention Meditation

"Energy flows where your attention goes." You hear that expression in every yoga studio and every meditation class at one time or another, and it's really true. If you mentally envision yourself achieving a goal, you're 50 percent there — just ask any pro athlete. On the flip side, one of the biggest hurdles to success is the belief that you can't do it. With intention meditation, you're removing that hurdle by mentally clearing the path. If meditation is the main act, intention setting is the foreplay that gets the energy going in the desired direction to make things happen.

Guided imagery and visualization are particularly good for setting intentions. I love how Unplug teacher and certified hypnotherapist Amy Budden explains this:

Guided Visualization meditation is a powerful way to use the mind to influence the body. It can also be an empowering way to manifest desired outcomes in your life. You can change your emotional or physical state by imagining it is so. For instance, one can imagine soothing warmth to diffuse discomfort or imagine vibrant health or energy when fatigued. Your body follows your mind's direction.

Try this: When you are tired and lack energy, repeat: *I am energized* over and over and visualize and imagine it. Use all your senses to make it real. Imagine the most energized you have ever felt. By visualizing, you begin to elicit these things both mentally and physically and you change your state. Within five minutes, I guarantee that you will feel better than you did when you started.

Intention + Visualization + Meditation = Results!

When you quiet yourself down, you connect to your soul and are able to hear and see what it wants. You can ask yourself some questions and find out what you truly desire. You may be surprised to find that something pops up that is completely different from what you thought you wanted.

To set an intention, begin by closing your eyes and taking a few slow, extended breaths. Then ask yourself: *What's the one thing I am most proud of accomplishing last year?* Whatever pops up first is usually your most intuitive answer. Really envision that accomplishment — how it felt, what it looked like, how you made it happen.

Then, ask yourself a second question: *What's the one thing I want to accomplish this year?* Imagine yourself achieving it as though it is happening in real time: how it looks, how it feels, how your life is changed as a result.

Then let it go, and begin your meditation. The point isn't to focus on your intention, but just to see it fully realized in your mind just before you slip into meditation, when your brain becomes more open and malleable.

Imagine your intention, let it go, breathe, meditate . . . and then go conquer the world!

More Practices to Try

When I first got into meditation I was all about keeping it simple, but the more I meditate, the more I want to explore other spiritual pathways. I find that the deeper I dive into myself, the deeper I get to dive into life. Once you get a taste of it, you just want to keep going!

Listed below are some other creative forms of meditation I have fallen in love with:

Tapping

You may have heard about tapping and wondered what the heck it is. From the outside, it definitely can look a little strange, even cultish, but it's actually one of the most powerful ways to initiate changes in your habits or thoughts.

Our teacher Lena George is an Advanced EFT (Emotional Freedom Technique)/tapping practitioner. I'm going to turn this over to her to explain exactly what tapping is, how it works, and how to do it:

The easiest way to understand tapping is to think of it as acupressure for the emotions. What we're doing is tapping with our fingertips on the specific energy points that are used in acupuncture, while at the same time saying out loud certain statements or issues we're working on. You're triggering the issue with your words, to bring it up, and then the tapping sends a calming signal through the connective tissue, which reframes and reprocesses your reactions to that trigger.

The verbalizing part is important. When you voice a trigger — like, say, a fear of public speaking — your whole system goes through a physiological response. When you tap, you send a calming signal at the same time you're bringing up that trigger, so they become de-linked in your brain. This works for everything from freeing yourself from sugar cravings to complex post-traumatic stress disorder issues.

I can attest to this — I've personally tapped out my cravings. Like a lot of people, my weakness is sugary carbs. I love cereal and can eat multiple bowls of it, or I'll just grab handfuls straight out of the box. Oh, and cookies . . . I never met one I didn't like. But tapping with Lena helped me stop eating these things for a solid eight days. (I broke down on day nine when faced with my son's birthday cake, but I plan to resume tapping so I can stay with it for good!) So many people love tapping because it truly does give tangible results that can change your life.

You can find a tapping practitioner by searching the directory at thetapping solution.com/eft-practitioners/. Or, you can also do it yourself at home by going to un plugmeditation.com for Lena's instructional video.

Crystal Healing

A lot of people think crystal healing sounds like the hokiest thing on the planet, but I've met people who swear their lives have been changed by it. And judging from how our students look before and after they go into the meditation studio for a crystal healing class, I have to say there is definitely some-thing to it. I see people going in stressed out and emerging totally calm and smiling.

The power of crystals basically comes down to vibration. All our internal organs vibrate on frequencies, and, according to

CHAKRA	LOCATION	ENERGY	COLOR	CRYSTAL
1st (root)	Base of the spine	Grounding, survival, protection	Red	Hematite, black tourmaline, red jasper
2nd (sacral)	Between the navel and the pubic bone	Sensuality, creative energy, courage	Orange	Orange calcite (gentle), carnelian (potent)
3rd (solar plexus)	Midsection	Personal power, abundance	Yellow	Citrine
4th (heart)	Center of the chest	Love, trust	Green	Rose quartz, green adventurine, green serpentine
5th (throat)	Throat area	Communication, self-expression	Blue	Blue lace agate, sodalite, chrysocolla, lapis lazuli
6th (third eye)	Between the eyebrows	Intuition, ideas, thoughts, dreams	Indigo	Amethyst
7th (crown)	Crown of the head, or slightly above it	Enlightenment, higher consciousness	Violet	Clear quartz, amethyst

certified crystal healers, putting the stones on various places on your body balances the frequencies that are out of whack. The stones tune you up, kind of like a guitar. Here's how crystal healer Jona Genova explains it:

It's actually very scientific, even though there's something magical about how it all comes together. Everything is a vibration. Even a table that looks solid is vibrating; we have scientific tools that can measure that. And vibrations respond to one another. Crystals vibrate at a fairly stable frequency. Because molecules tend to mirror one another when they get close, when these stable crystals are placed near the unstable frequencies of our bodies, they bring them into balance. That means that just by being near crystals, they're going to heal us.

Crystal healing is what's known as "passive meditation," meaning you just relax completely and give over to the healing properties of the crystals. There's no focusing on the breath or anything else in crystal healing. The only goal is to feel and be receptive. Or, as Jona puts it, "[l]et the crystal meditate you."

In Jona's class, she has each person choose three to four crystals that they feel drawn toward intuitively. After a brief guided meditation, she places your crystals on the chakras (energy points) on your body as needed. Many people report feeling vibrations, pulsing, waves like energy, or heat or coolness emanating from the stones. Afterward, they describe feeling lighter, more aligned, clearer, and peaceful but energized at the same time. Basically, exactly how you want to feel.

But don't worry if you don't know of a good crystal healer or class nearby — you can also do this yourself. Here's the how-to:

1. Choose a crystal that you feel drawn to. Remember, it's best to choose it in person, so you can touch and feel it.
2. Once you've chosen your crystal, if you like, you can learn a little bit about the properties it promotes (love, calmness, grounding, etc.).
3. Lie down and place your crystal on a part of your body that you feel needs it most. If you're not sure where, take a look at the chart on page 200 for help in choosing the

chakra that your stone best corresponds to. If the stone you've chosen isn't on this list, you can easily look up the best chakra for it online.

4. Relax, breathe, and tune in to the crystal. You don't need to do anything other than absorb its vibrations. Just lie there, breathing in and out, noticing which chakras you feel the most. Usually, one will feel more dominant; for me, it's often the throat chakra. That's the one that probably needs the most attention in your life. Then let go of anything you noticed and relax and breathe some more. If you don't feel anything, that's okay, too; you will get the benefits even without the awareness. Try to do this for a minimum of ten minutes each time to really experience it. Thirty minutes to an hour is even better.

Once you've done this a few times with your crystal, you build a relationship with it. Then go try a different crystal. You'll experience the contrast and get a sense of the nuances of each individual stone. Keep going, trying out different crystals, and build a collection of your favorites.

The easiest way to balance the chakras using crystals is to choose a stone whose color matches the chakra color. For an easy way to remember the corresponding color, just think *ROYGBIV* — the colors of the rainbow — as you'll see below. Or, you can choose stones that are known to work best for each chakra (which may or may not match in color). I've included a few of the top ones for each chakra in the chart.

Breath Work

People *love* breath work. It's a great way to release stuck energy — and I now know what that actually means! I used to hear "release stuck energy" and think, *What energy, and where is it stuck?* Now I get that we store energy in our body but often never release it. It's similar to holding in your words when you want to scream. Breath work lets you open up the Pandora's box and let it go so you can move on.

Breath work also prepares you to fully relax into meditation. You exhaust yourself, emotionally and physically, which puts you into this place of utter stillness and calm. It's the same with yoga — did you know that the whole purpose of yoga poses is to move out stuck energy and exhaust the body so you can be still in meditation/savasana (the full-body relaxation pose) at the end? It's true.

I'm going to turn this over to one of our amazing breath work teachers, Jon Paul Crimi. Jon Paul's classes fill up in a matter of minutes, and people swear it's changed their life. Here's Jon Paul on what breath work is and why it's so powerful:

Breath work is an incredible tool to get you to a place of quiet, which works well for people who have a hard time sitting still and meditating. The experience is like a workout, only using your breath. Basically, you're breathing through your mouth in an intensified way, which activates the sympathetic nervous system — the fight-or-flight response — and immediately puts you into the present moment. But because you're doing it in a safe environment, it has the effect of releasing stuck trauma. Things that have happened to you that you don't even realize are still in there will come up and out.

The first ten minutes can be tough, like a workout. Some people get dizzy the first couple of times they do breath work, but that passes after a few minutes. I always remind people: "You're lying down, so you're not going to pass out! If you're willing to push through that and stick with it, you will have a massive and profound experience." It has undeniable effects and results. One thing I hear a lot is "It's like a year of therapy in one class or session!"

It's best to do breath work with an experienced teacher. Yoga studios are often a good source to ask for recommendations for teachers.

I'm a left-brainer and a management consultant. I typically wouldn't have the time or patience for meditation. Truthfully, my doctor told me I should because my stress and cholesterol were high. When I went to see a holistic practitioner rather than start taking statins, I got a whole new lease on life. That led me to my first breath work class. Game over — I was hooked. Best drug ever!

TED, 50, MANAGEMENT CONSULTANT

Sound Baths

If you've never tried a sound bath, you definitely should!

A sound bath is a deep meditative experience in which a practitioner uses gongs, bells, bowls, drums, and other instruments to create an immersive experience. I love them because they are so all-encompassing. Your body is cradled and wrapped in sound, so it's very comforting and soothing. Just lying there and feeling the vibrations against your body literally bangs the stress right out of you.

On Saturday nights, we're lucky enough to have Guy Douglas, who is one of the best sound bath healers in the business, come do a sound bath at Unplug. The room is always packed for this utterly cool experience; it completely envelops you and transports you out of your head and into the healing vibration of sound.

Here's Guy's explanation of what sound baths are and how they work:

A sound bath is a sound meditation experience that uses sound to cancel out the mind chatter and bring you to the zero point of meditation. NASA has done recordings of outer space, and the sounds you hear from gongs and bowls sound very much like it; they align you with that primal, infinite energy. They allow you to go into a deep level of just being, which is great for people who may not be used to meditating yet. The harmonious layers of vibration take you out of the ego mind and put you in direct connection with your true self. The vibrations clear the channels of all the stuff that gets stagnant within us so we can get to our wisdom and truth — whatever that is for each one of us. It sounds far out, but it's really like that!

Sound baths also heal us. Music has been used for thousands of years in cultures from all over the world for healing; think church bells, or Native American drums. The acoustic tones and frequencies of a sound bath cause a sympathetic vibration that affects us on a deep cellular level.

Many yoga studios host sound baths, and you can find one pretty easily in most cities. You have to be careful who you do a sound bath with, however, because there is such a thing as a bad one. It should be soothing, not jarring. What I love about Guy's in particular is that he's a talented musician, not just someone banging on things and blowing out your eardrums. So be sure to do a little research to see if the practitioner you're considering is any good.

Meditation for Kids

You can hear all the science and experience all the phenomenal changes within yourself, but when you see meditation at work in your child, it takes it to a whole other level.

Sitting still and breathing isn't something that sounds particularly fun to kids, and most have to be talked into trying it. I can honestly say that talking my boys into it is one of the best things I've done as a parent. All three of them tried meditation reluctantly, but once they sat down and did it, they liked it (kind of like a lot of adults I know). Do they practice now every day? Not at all. But do they know how to use it on demand, as a tool to self-regulate when they need it? Absolutely. When I used to tell my son to turn off the Xbox, he'd throw a fit and toss the clicker at me. Now he takes three breaths and just walks off. So much better than flinging electronic equipment, right? If my meditation studio burned down tomorrow, it would have all been worth it just for that!

I asked Laurie Cousins, who teaches our kids meditation classes, to explain why it's such a beneficial practice for kids. Here's what she had to say:

Meditation can be a wonderful tool to help children regulate themselves emotionally, to be less impulsive, and to bring their attention to something they want to focus on rather than being distracted. It teaches them to breathe when they're feeling anxious, and to see their anger and work with it in that moment. It helps them get in touch with their body, and their heart. They can find a sense of kindness and connection to themselves and others, which helps in their social relationships.

It's very helpful for middle and high school students, specifically. They understand the sense of self and self-consciousness; to be able to be aware of their inner dialogue is so valuable. The more they tune in and explore this relationship with themselves, the more they can hear their own wisdom and insights and choose actions that are helpful to them as opposed to carrying out unconscious habits that are not.

I see it all the time: children being able to turn to themselves in a healthy way versus seeking unhealthy ways to manage what feels unmanageable. With the stressors, structure, and expectations that go along with being a kid today, meditation gives them ways to slow down and identify that they're stressed, that there's pressure, and to choose how to attend to it in a helpful way.

There are two "tricks" to getting your kids to meditate. The first is to live by example. As Laurie says, "Kids watch what we do more than what we say. If they see us taking the time to pause and breathe and do something that is quiet — or even just focusing on one thing at a time, consciously — they will observe and want to do it, too. As soon as we impose it on them, they feel our agenda and don't want to do it."

The other way to get your kids to meditate is to make it fun. Try short, guided meditations, or even a walking meditation if they're super high-energy. To most kids, words like *calm* and *stillness* sound like torture. There are so many great meditations for kids out there, but here are my three favorite to get you started:

Meditation in a Jar
This meditation is a great visual tool to show kids how their brain works when they're amped up versus when they're calm. Plus, it's sparkly and tactile — two things most kids love. Here's how to do it:

1. Fill a ball jar with water and glitter. I'm partial to purple glitter, but use any color they love. Be sure to screw the top on tight.
2. Explain how the mind is a jar and that the glitter represents thoughts and feelings.
3. Shake it up and explain how this is what the mind looks like when you are angry, or in a hurry, or stressed.
4. Ask your child to slowly breathe in and out along with you, and show them how when we breathe, everything settles and becomes clear — just like the water in the jar.

The Calm Down a Crying Child Meditation
This meditation comes from Susan Kaiser Greenland, the author of the highly acclaimed book *The Mindful Child.* Susan is considered one of the leading teachers of mindful awareness for kids and teens. This meditation comes from her acclaimed Inner Kids program, and is a brilliantly sneaky way to get your child to slow down their breath and get calm:

1. Have your child imagine that they are standing in a garden filled with beautiful roses. Tell them to smell

the flowers around them, inhaling through their nose as long as they can.

2. Next, have them place their pointer finger out in front of them at arm's length. Tell them to imagine their finger is a candle and to blow gently to make the flame flicker. The goal isn't to blow out the candle, but to exhale slowly and gently for as long as possible.

Do this ten times and watch the shift.

The Go to Sleep Already Meditation
This is another Susan Kaiser Greenland meditation that is frequently taught by Laurie Cousins, who runs our kids program. It takes the torture and stress out of bedtime and turns it into a calming routine that kids really respond to. Do this practice for three minutes and they'll slip into sleepytime like magic.

1. Ask your child to choose a favorite stuffed animal.
2. With your child lying down in bed, place the stuffed animal on their belly.
3. Have them watch the animal rise

and fall as they breathe in and out.
The thoughts and worries of the
day will disappear as they focus on
their toy and breathe.

THE ULTIMATE SECRET OF MEDITATION

There is a way to take your practice to the next level . . . to go deeper . . . to journey into the depths of your soul and into your higher consciousness beyond anything you've experienced. This is the secret that sages, monks, and yogis from ancient to modern times know. It is the step that takes their practice from powerful to mind-blowingly extraordinary. And now I'm going to share it with you.

Ready?

Just do it more for longer periods of time.

Really. That's it.

Students ask Davidji all the time for the "advanced technique" of meditation, but as he says, *This is it!* This is all there is. The way you go bigger and dive deeper is just by sustaining your practice and doing it a little longer, and a little more often.

Consistency is key. I know it can be easy to fall off the meditation wagon, especially

when you feel like you've gotten the positive results that you were looking for when
you first started this journey. But I also
know that when I fall off, I can slip right
back into my old habits. So I stay with it,
because the results are so worth it. When I
meditate, everything is just better.

A little every day goes a long way, and the
longer you sit in stillness, the deeper and
more fulfilling your life will be. Five minutes
can make a profound difference in your day,
and in your life. But, when it comes to
meditation, more is definitely better. Once
you get comfortable, try sitting for ten
minutes. Or twenty, or forty-five. Or go big
and try a silent retreat — I did this and it
was transformative! Think double black
diamond of meditation.

The best way to get to twenty minutes a
day is to work your way up to it. Try the
Unplug 28-Day Meditation Challenge to
get you there:

Week One: Sit daily for 1 to 5 minutes
Week Two: Sit daily for 5 to 10 minutes
Week Three: Sit daily for 10 to 15 minutes
Week Four: Sit daily for 15 to 20 minutes

When you meditate twenty-eight days in a
row, your brain transforms and your whole

world shifts right along with it. Will all your problems go away? No. But your response to them will make them a lot less important. You'll have the power to take yourself on an inner vacation at any time, and to find your passion, your purpose, and your peace. What makes you happy? What do you need to let go of? Why are you here? How do you want to live your life? These are the questions that are answered when you unplug, sit in silence, and meditate.

So unplug for a few minutes each day . . . and then a few more . . . and a few more. Then just keep going. You got this!

RESOURCES

Please visit unplugmeditation.com to learn more about ways to explore all the types of meditation you've read about here. There you'll find videos, tutorials, blog posts, products, and more. And if you're in the Los Angeles area, please come visit the Unplug studio. I'd love to see you there!

ACKNOWLEDGMENTS

My first acknowledgment really must go to my mom, Ina Yalof, who has always told me that I could do anything I set my mind to, except for this book (LOL). When I told her I wanted to write a book, she, who herself has written fourteen, explained to me that there was no way I could do this alone, with a husband, three small children, and a start-up business. So she gave me a gift: She introduced me to her legendary agent, Richard Pine, who made this book happen with effortless ease.

A few days later, Richard was having lunch with Doris Cooper, editor of my first book, *Getting Over John Doe,* when she suggested he place the book in the hands of my talented and very perceptive editor Diana Baroni, who loved the idea and whose enthusiasm and mission for sharing this story with the world made it a dream project. I feel so fortunate that this book landed with her. The happy connections kept going when Richard hooked me up with talented writer Debra Goldstein, who became my collaborator and my new best friend. While working on this book, Debra — who had never meditated before — and I spent a year taking classes together, listening to podcasts, and continually e-mailing back and forth. She ultimately became a dedicated meditator and, as a result, was able to help me create a book that perfectly addressed the needs of beginning students.

This book would never have existed without the love and dedication of many brilliant teachers, the first of whom was my mother-in-law, Linda Schwartz, who showed me how to breathe, visualize, and calm myself down — all in a matter of minutes. My dear friend Jennifer Schiff helped me write my business plan at our kitchen table and came up with the name *Unplug.* The guidance of the iconic yogi Steve Ross — author of *Happy Yoga,* owner of Maha Yoga in LA, and my meditation and business guru — was instrumental. Steve's philosophy of "If we can get more people doing this, the world will be a better place" has since become my mantra and the guiding reason I do what I do.

My deepest appreciation to the following

people who have guided and taught me and changed my life in more ways than they will ever know: Olivia Rosewood, Davidji, Natalie Bell, Deepak Chopra, Mallika Chopra, and Megan Monahan. And thanks also to the Unplug meditation teachers and guest teachers who contributed to this book: Susan Kaiser Greenland, Laurie Cousins, Scott Schwenk, Johnny O'Callaghan, Lauren Eckstrom, Tracee Stanley, Sara Ivanhoe, Lena George, Amy Budden, Harry Paul, Heather Hayward, Jona Genova, Guy Douglas, Kelly Barron, Danielle Beinstein, Jon Paul Crimi, Ben Decker, Camilla Sacre-Dallerup, Jane Garnett, Christina Huntington, David Elliott, Carrie Keller, Paul Teodo, Sherly Sulaiman, Lili Pettit, Ali Owens, Donna D'Cruz, Stefanie Goldstein, PhD, Ananda Giri, Jessica Snow, Laura Conley, Angela Whittaker, Light Watkins, Arianna Huffington, Agapi Stassinopoulos, Danna Weiss, Dean Sluyter, Dr. Belisa Vranich, Felicia Tomasko, Jonathan Beaudette, Kristen Luman, Aimee Bello, Peter Oppermann, Sally Kempton. I am grateful, also, to Harvard/Mass General neuroscientist Sara Lazar and UCLA cardiologist Tamara Horwich for their medical wisdom and insight.

My incredible team at Unplug took over

when I had deadlines to meet. Thank you, Lisa Haase, Deborah Brock, McKayla Matthews, Sheryl Seifer, Suzy Shelton, Katie Burton, Charlie O'Connor, Anjani Joshi, Chelsea Scerri, Joe Chambrello, Gola Rakhshani, Scott Ishihara, Shannon Estabrook, Shayne Collins, Yaron Deskalo, Casey Altman, and Brendan Walters.

And, of course, a big thank-you to my friends and family who helped bring this book to fruition in ways small and large: Leslie Garfield, Stephen Yalof, Liora Yalof, Arthur Schwartz, Clarissa Potter, Ken Schwartz, Janie Liepshutz, Robin Berman, Christine Bernstein, Sam O'Conner, Lulu Powers, Inge Fonteyne, Heidi Krupp, Julie Rice, Elisabeth Cutler, Amy Peck, Lee Ann Sauter, Lisa Hersh, Beryl Weiner, Julie Cramer, and Christie Lowe. And to Emma Krasner: Thank you for loaning me your mom for a year.

High fives to my CEO in the sky, Herb Yalof. Dad, if you were still on this earth, I might never have had to search for the meaning in life.

Finally, to my husband, Marc, the most mindful human I know. You keep me grounded so I don't expand too far out into the universe. I am so grateful to have you not only on my team, but leading it. And to my munchkins, Austin, Tyler, and Cooper, who are now taller than me (except Cooper): Thank you for being smart, wild, crazy, fun, and loving and the reason why I needed to do this in the first place.

INDEX

ABOUT THE AUTHOR

Suze Yalof Schwartz is the founder and CEO of the popular Los Angeles–based meditation studio Unplug Meditation. For decades she was a fashion editor, director, and stylist at *Vogue, Elle, Marie Claire,* and *Glamour.* She has appeared on *Today, Good Morning America, The Early Show,* and the *View,* as well as on the *Oprah Winfrey Show* and CNN.